The
JAZZ GUITAR CHORD BIBLE
COMPLETE

by Warren Nunes

With Special Thanks To
JOEL HIPPS & STEVE DOHERTY

Also:
ED PASTERNAK
GEORGE COLE
RICHARD PARKER
BLACK BARON OF SAN JOAQUIN
JERRY MARCELLINO
DAVID SIEFF

Alfred Music
P.O. Box 10003
Van Nuys, CA 91410-0003
alfred.com

ISBN-10: 0-7692-7972-4
ISBN-13: 978-0-7692-7972-5

Contents:

Major Chords

Minor Chords

Major & Minor Chords

Dominant

FOREWORD

As a jazz guitarist I always have sought to help less experienced jazz musicians find practical solutions to their problems. This book should solve one of the greatest problems...the knowledge and use of chords.

Vol. 1 and Vol. 2 of the Chord Bible are a complete guide to three and four string guitar chords. Chords used for both comping and chorded solos are included. Every type of sound is covered, including passing chords and altered chords. Other chord voicings may be possible, but only THE MOST LOGICAL, PRACTICAL AND APPLICABLE CHORD VOICINGS ARE PRESENTED.

An example is presented for each chord voicing which shows one way the chord is used in a chord progression. Each chord is identified by a number next to the chord name. Turn to the example with the same number to see how the chord is used. Chords and examples are presented only in one key. Transpose the chords and examples to other keys, based on the chord analysis, using the harmonized scales and a guitar fingerboard chart for reference.

Many of the chords in this book do not have the root in the chord. To hear the complete chord, the root note should be sounded in the bass. Ask a friend to play the bass notes while you play the chords or "tape" the bass notes and play the examples along with your own recording.

WARREN NUNES

● EXPLANATION OF MUSICAL NOTATION

A   Chord symbol
B   Fret number
C   Finger number
D   Chord construction (intervals)
E   Chord notation
F   Number next to chord form indicates the
    corresponding example progression.

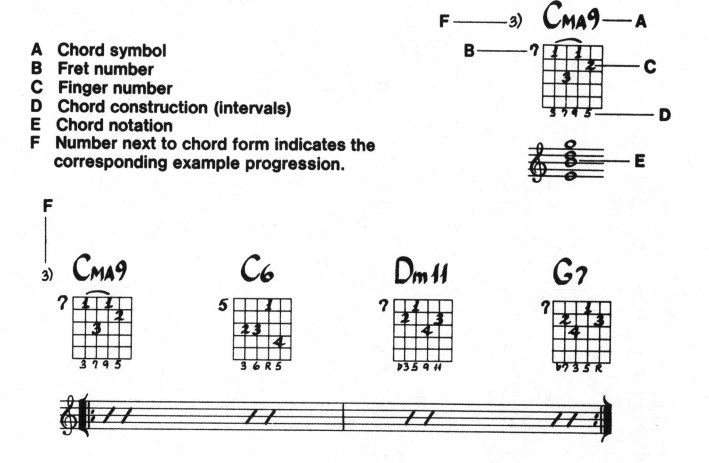

● EXPLANATION OF MUSICAL SYMBOLS

● CHORD NAME SYMBOL

Ma = major
m = minor
Ma7 = major 7
dim = diminished
+ = augmented
- = flatted (♭)

● CHORD CONSTRUCTION (INTERVALS) SYMBOLS

R = root
♭7 = dominant seventh
7 = major seventh

● FINGERING SYMBOLS

⌒   = barre the string

●BASIC MAJOR

● Keyboard Analysis:

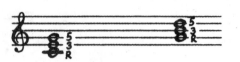

●● Have a friend play the root note in the bass in order to hear the complete chord.

CHORD FORMS

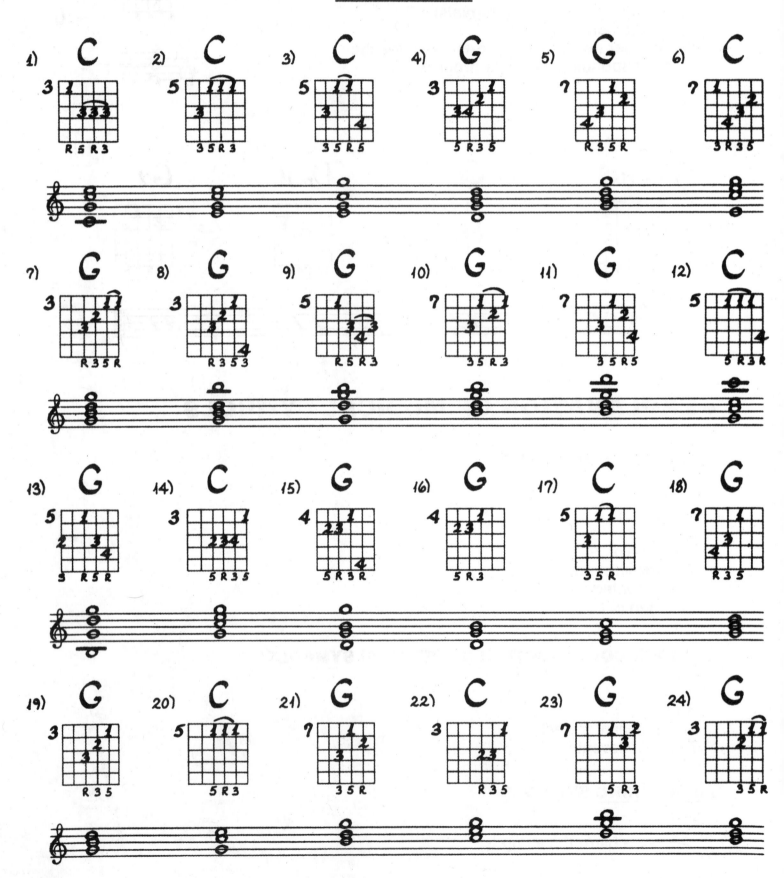

● BASIC MAJOR EXAMPLES

● ● Have a friend play the root note in the bass in order to hear the complete chord.

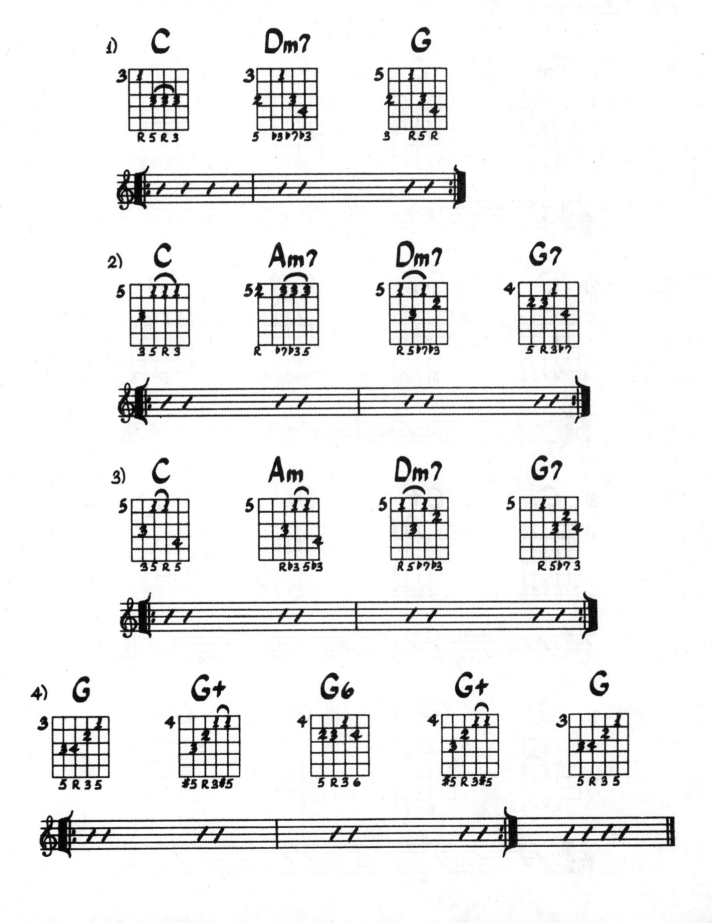

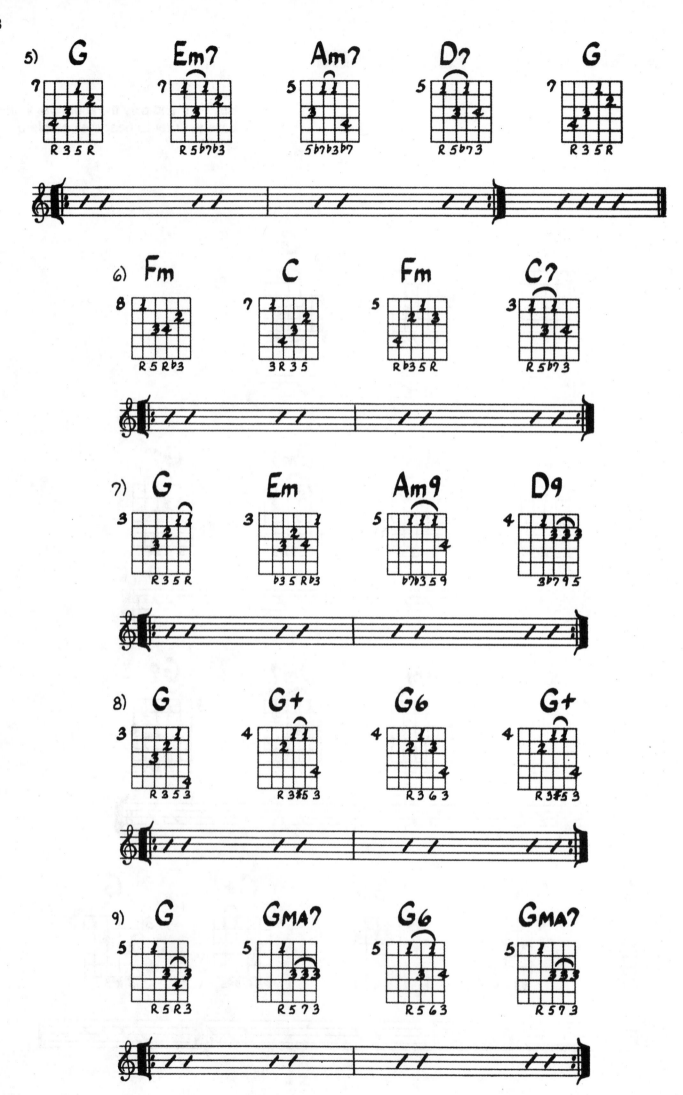

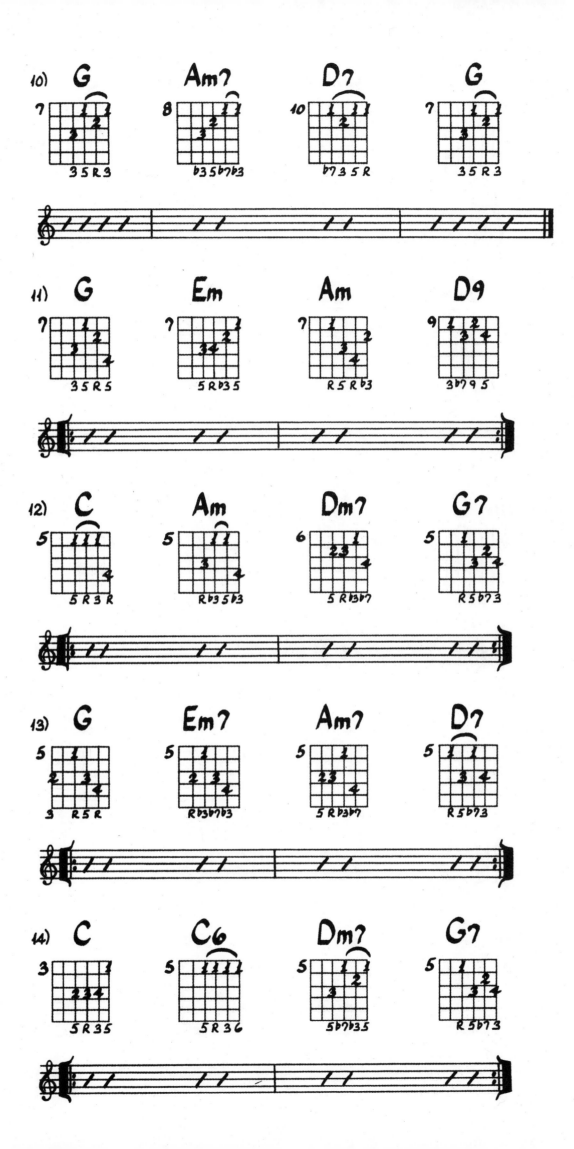

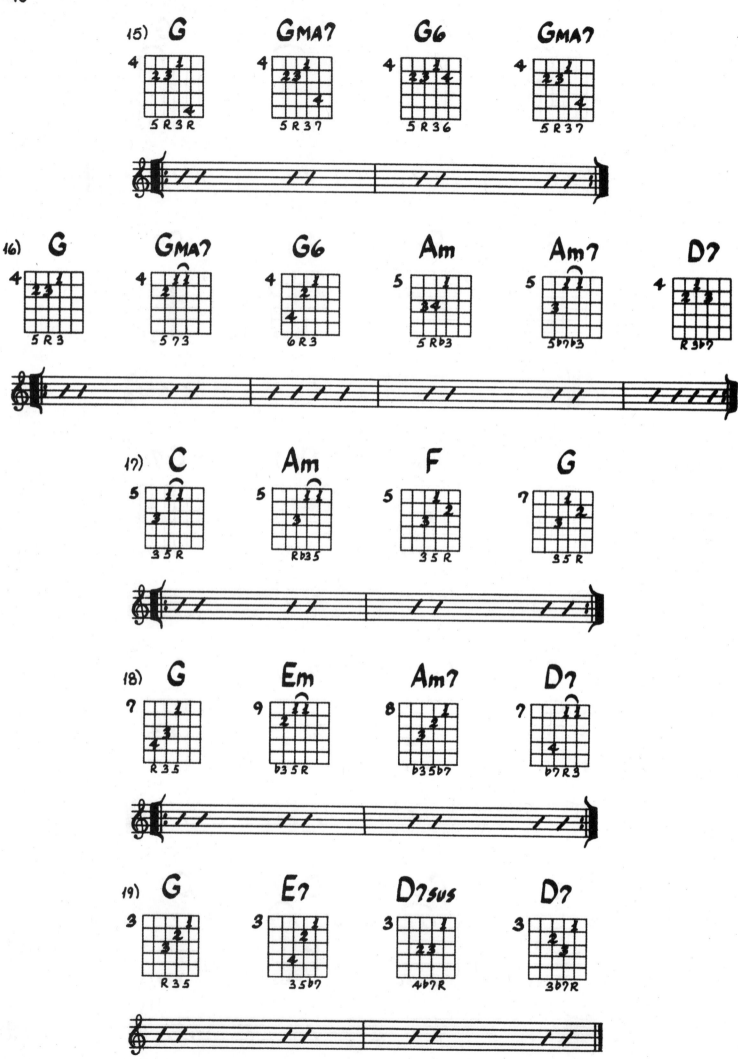

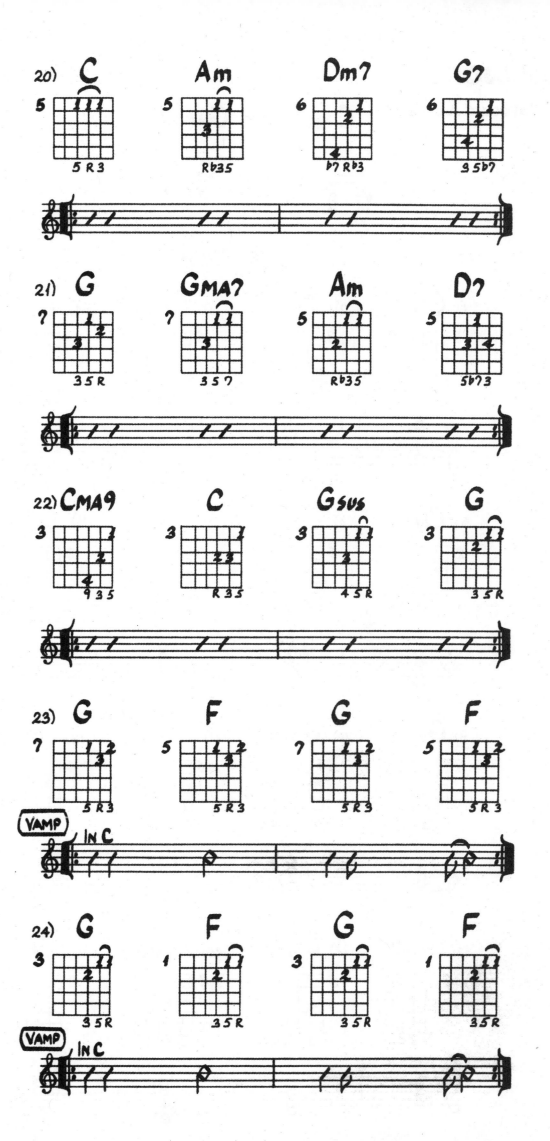

● MAJOR 7

● Keyboard Analysis:

CHORD FORMS

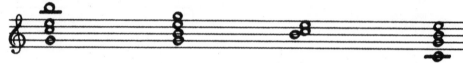

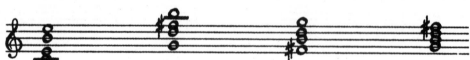

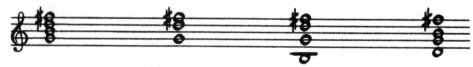

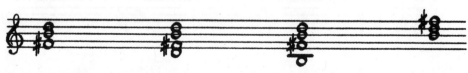

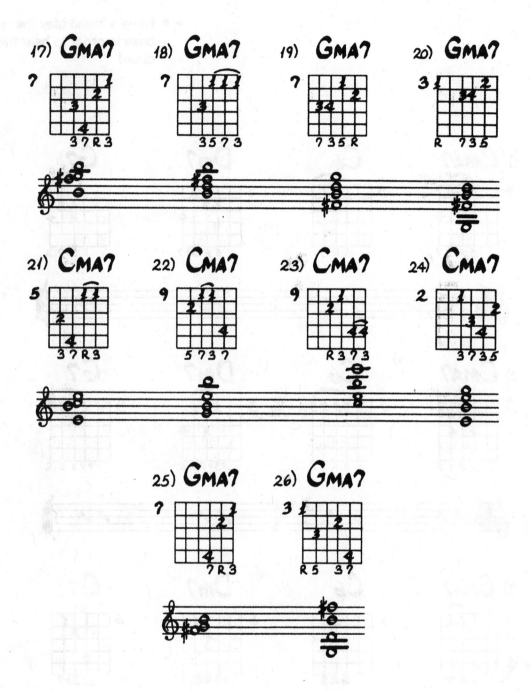

● MAJOR 7 EXAMPLES

● ● Have a friend play the root note in the bass in order to hear the complete chord.

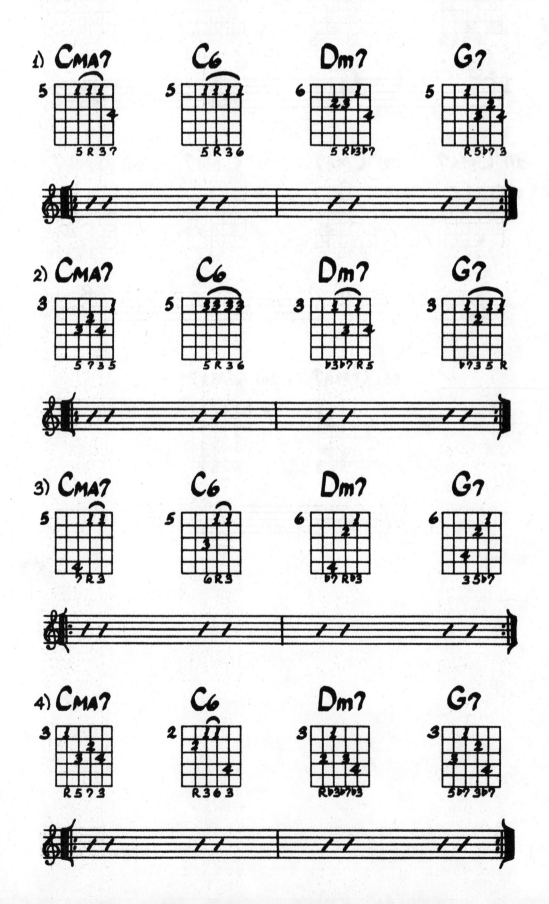

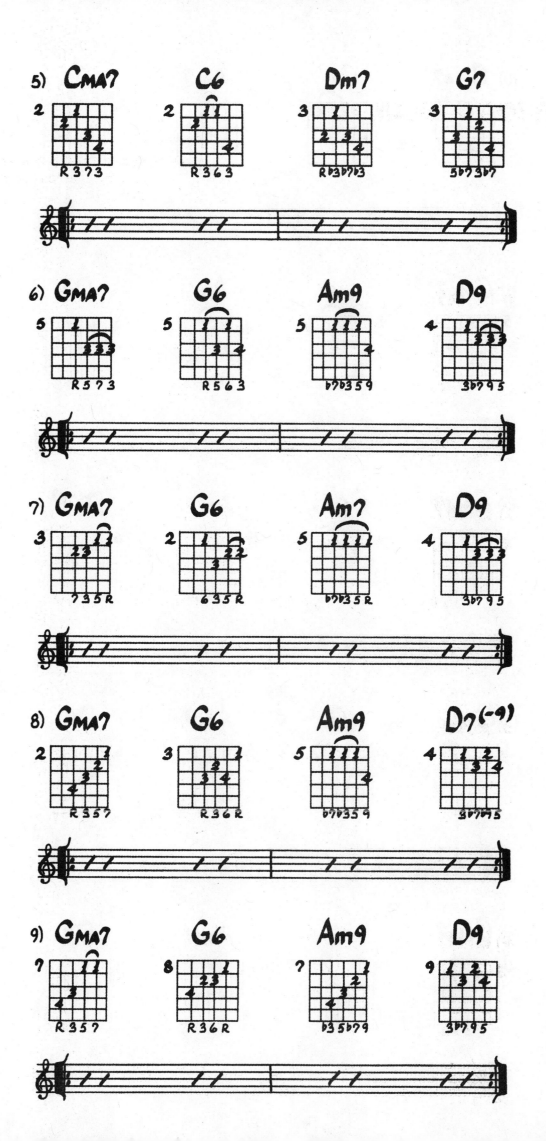

16

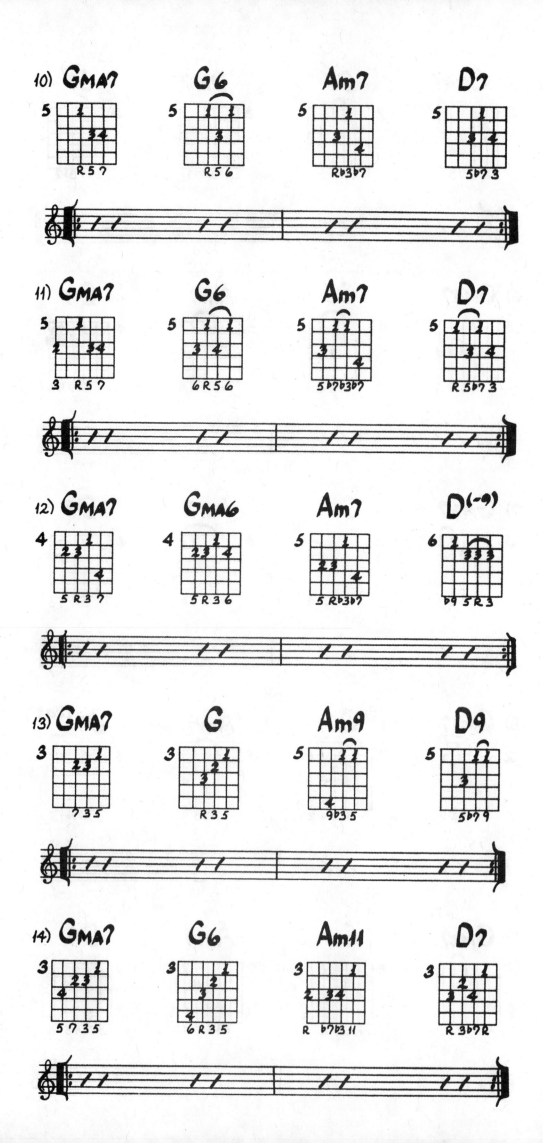

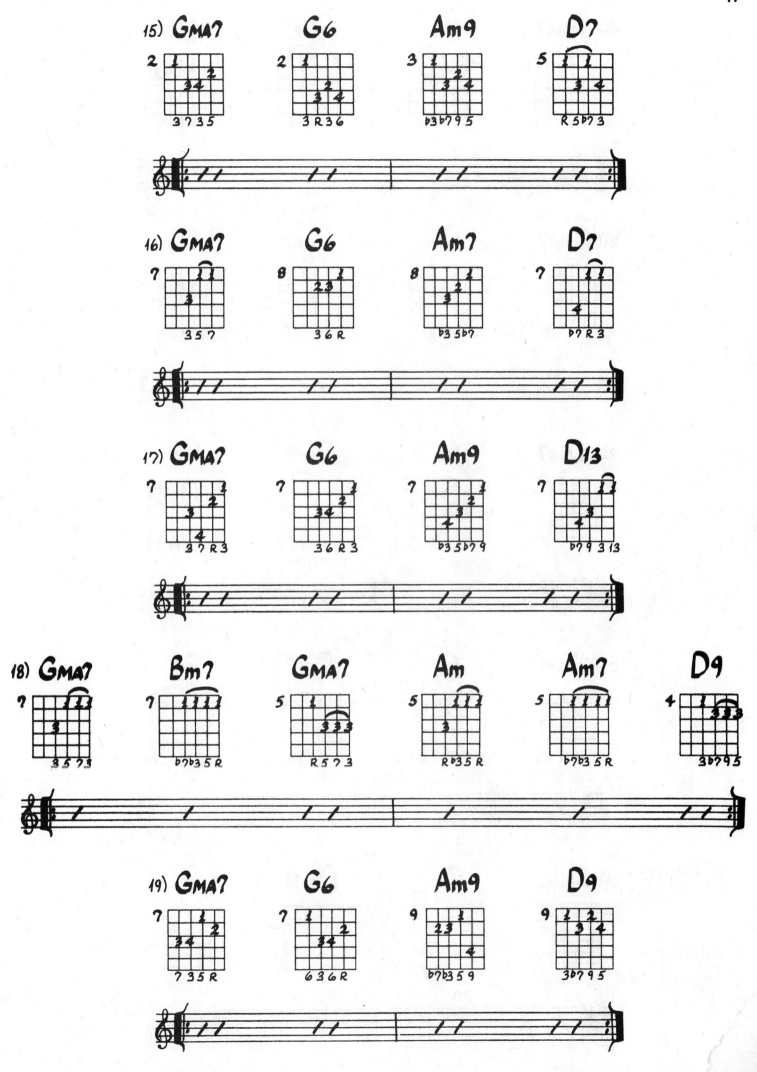

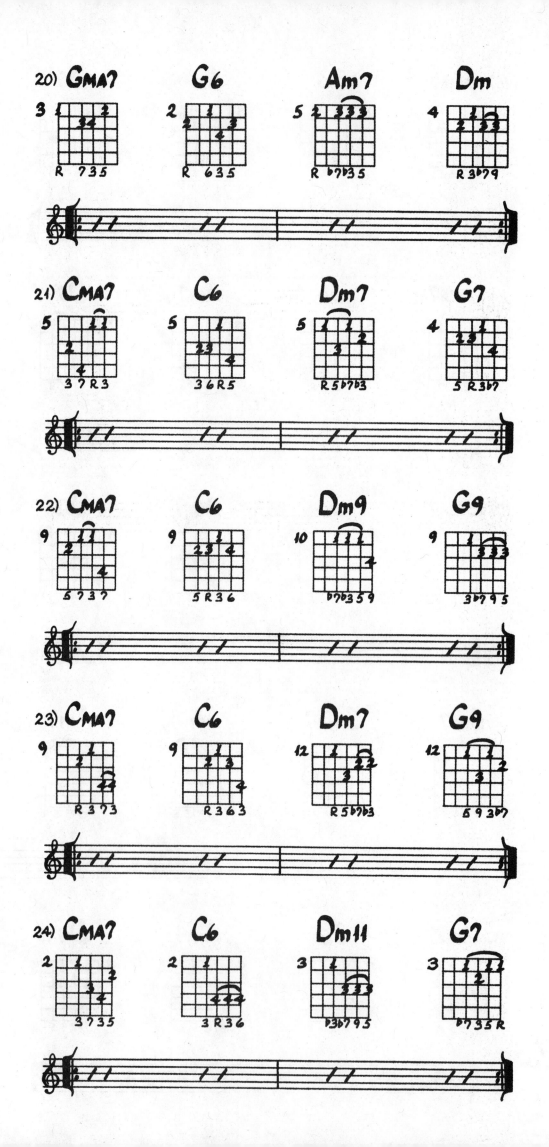

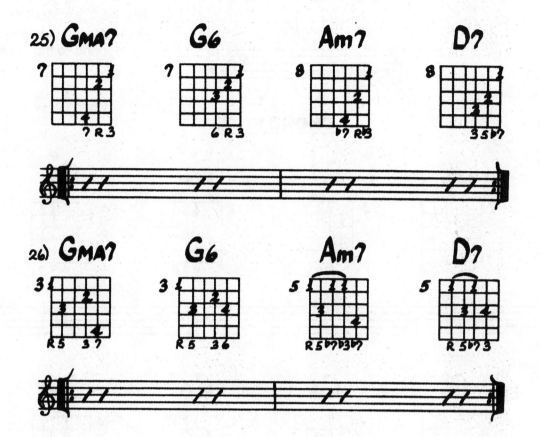

● MAJOR 6

● Keyboard Analysis:

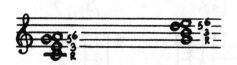

● ● See Ma7 and Ma9 for examples. The numbers for the Ma6 chords do not correspond to the example numbers.

CHORD FORMS

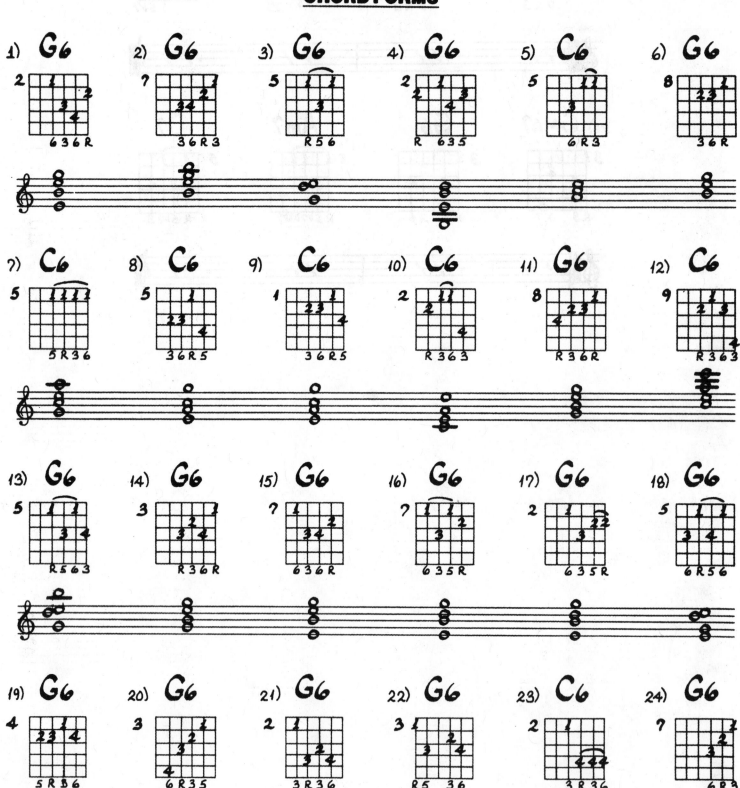

● MAJOR 9

● **Keyboard Analysis:**

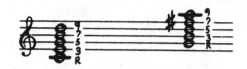

CHORD FORMS

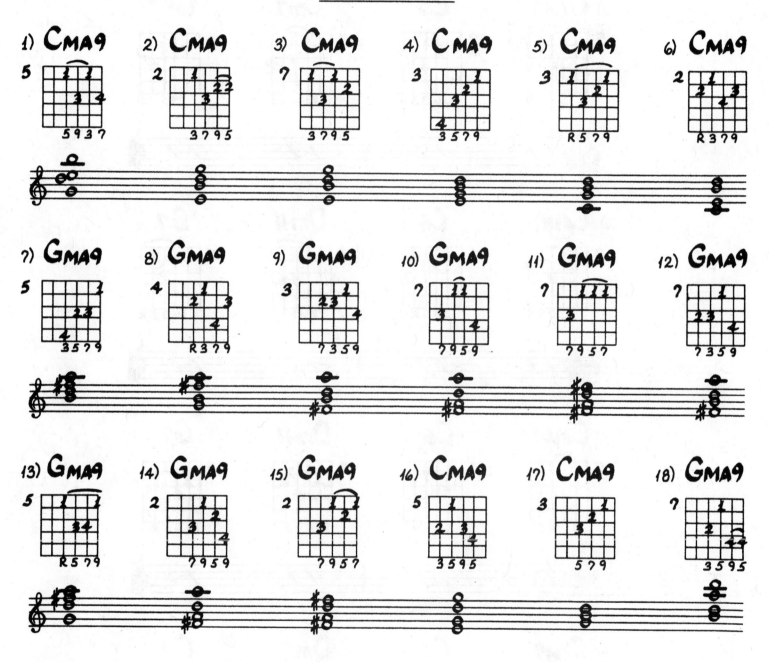

● MAJOR 9 EXAMPLES

● ● Have a friend play the root note in the bass in order to hear the complete chord.

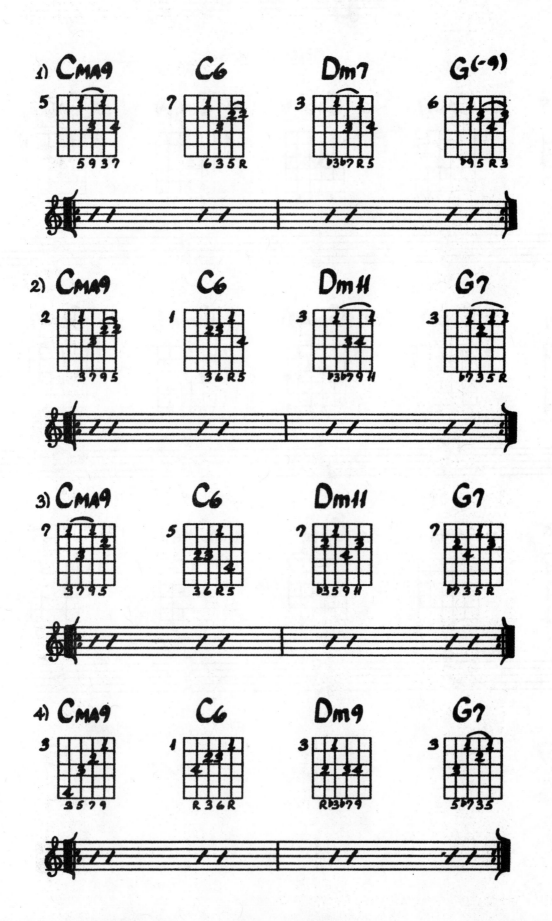

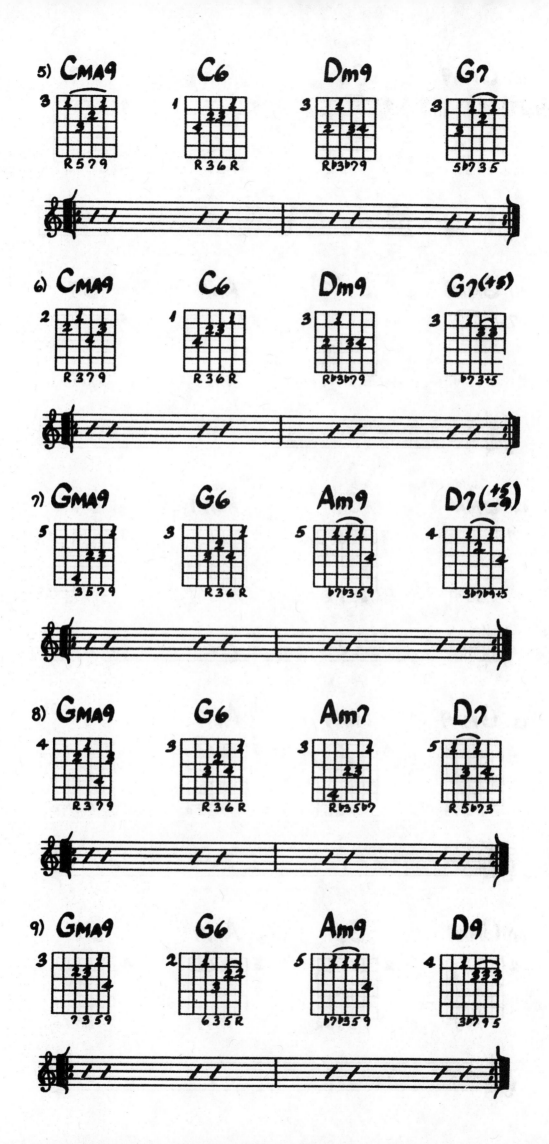

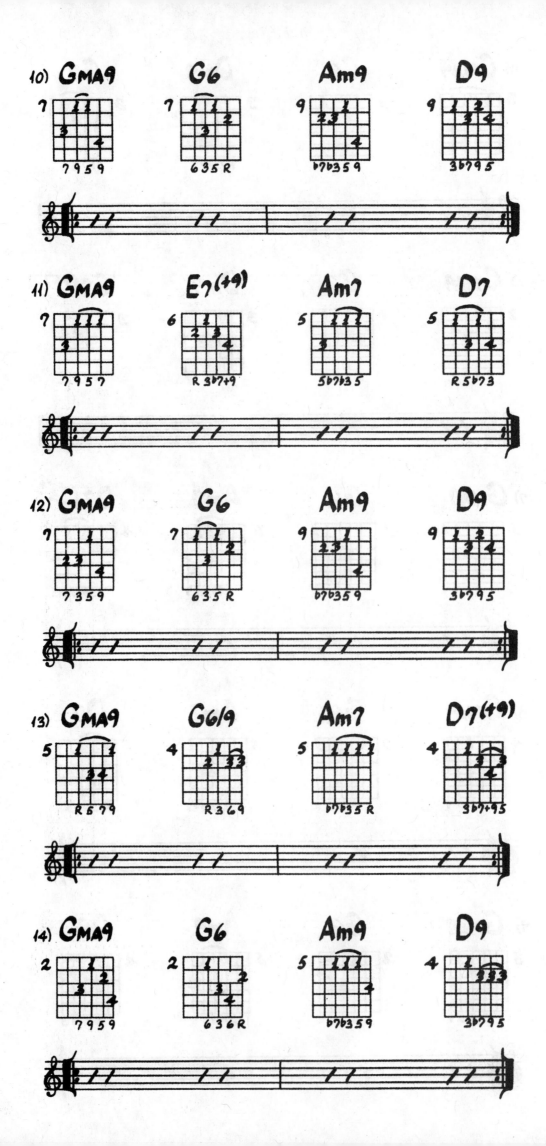

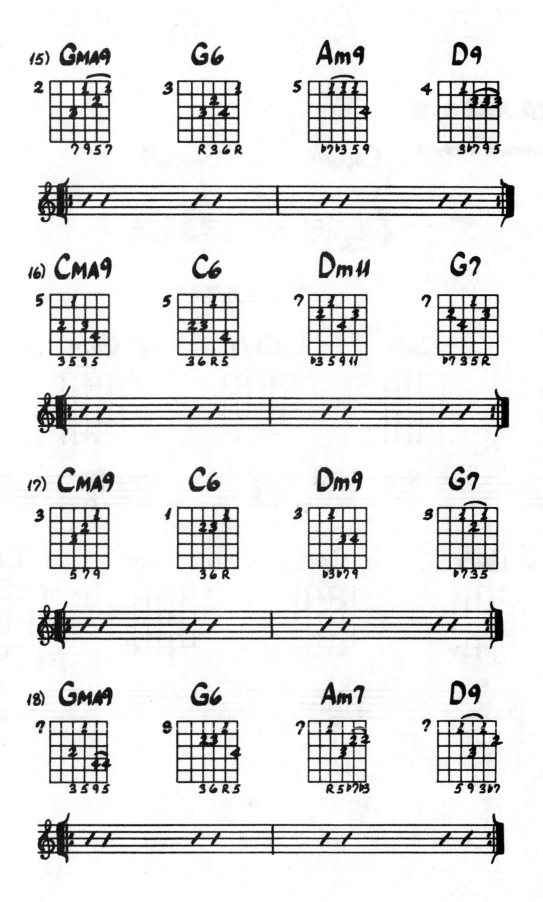

● MAJOR 6/9

● Keyboard Analysis:

CHORD FORMS

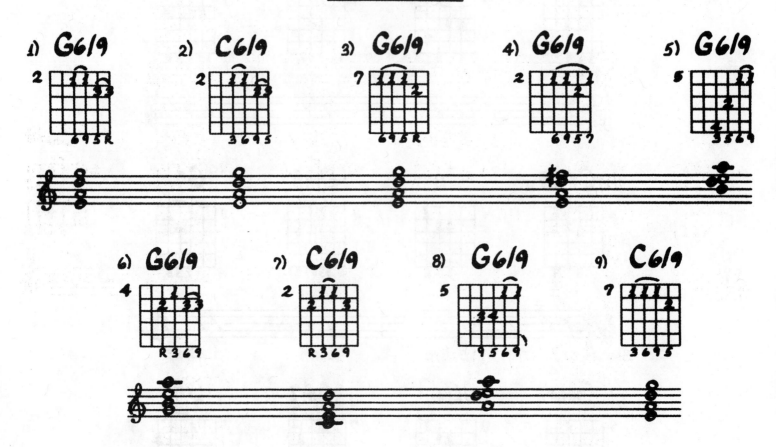

•MAJOR 6/9 EXAMPLES

• • Have a friend play the root note in the bass in order to hear the complete chord.

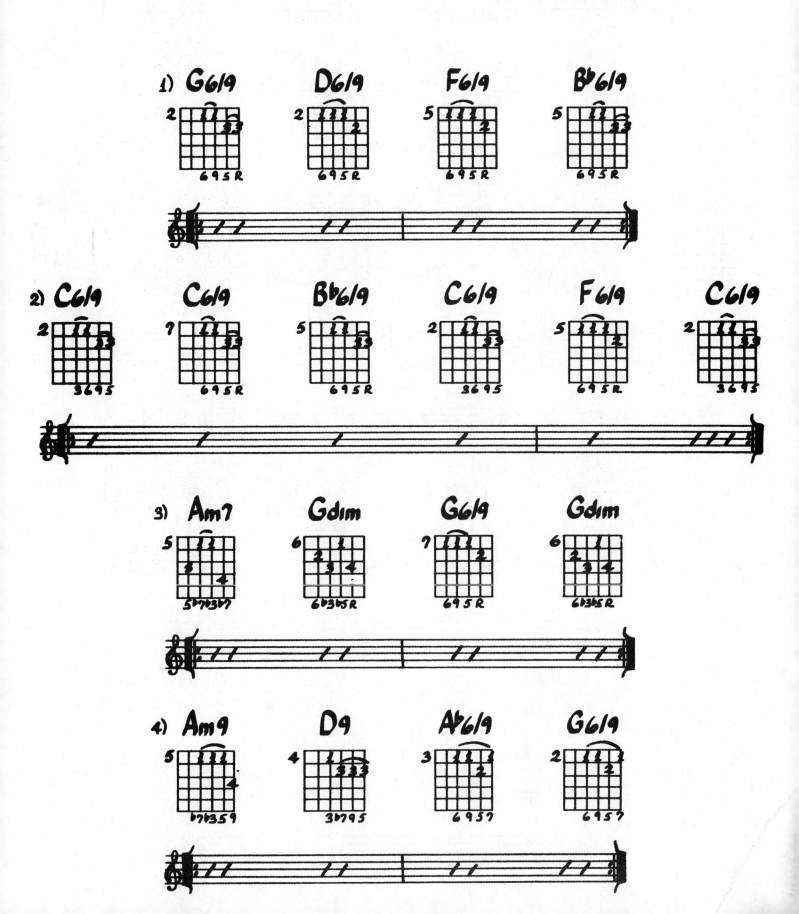

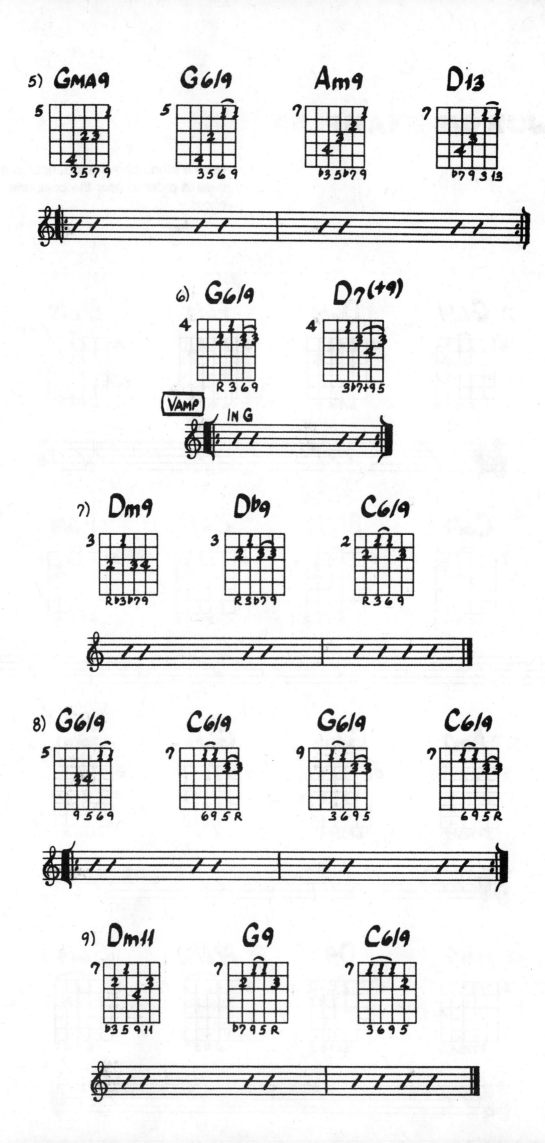

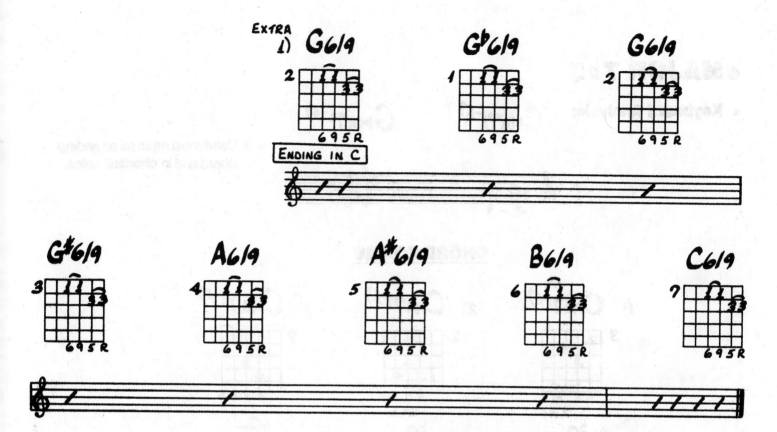

●MAJOR 7♭5

● **Keyboard Analysis:**

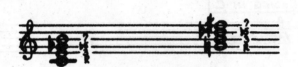

●● Used most often as an ending chord and in chorded solos.

CHORD FORMS

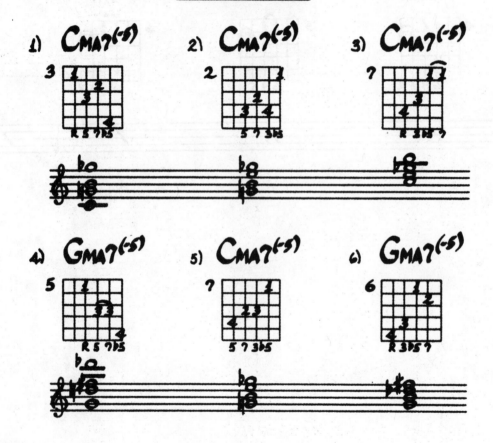

●MAJOR 7♭5 EXAMPLES

● ● Have a friend play the root note in the bass in order to hear the complete chord.

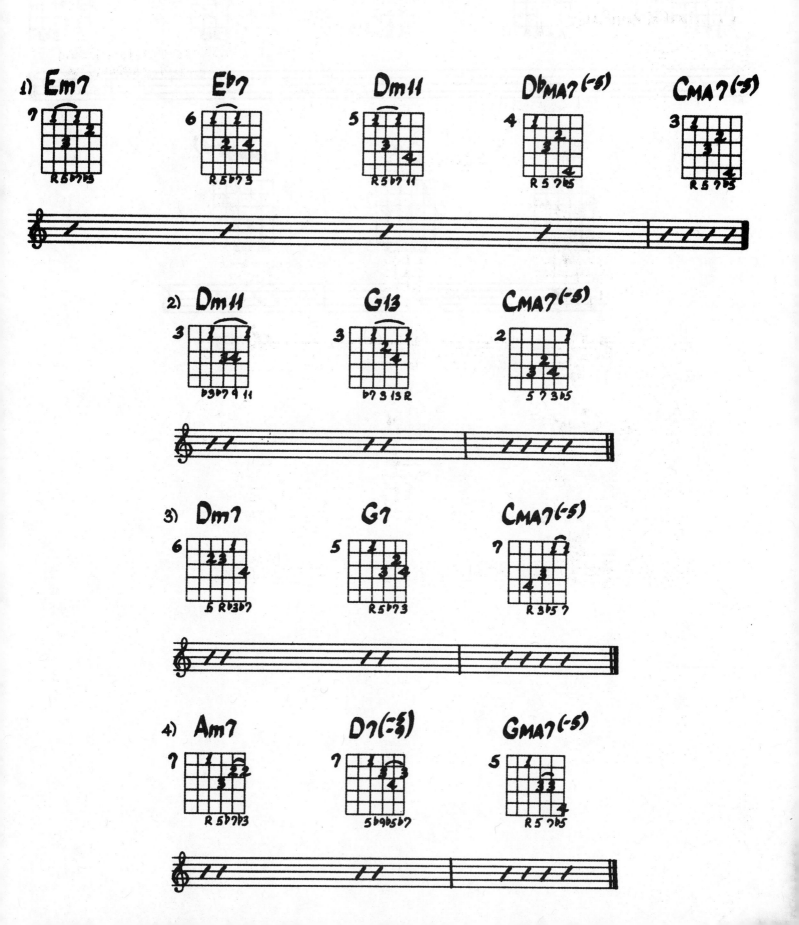

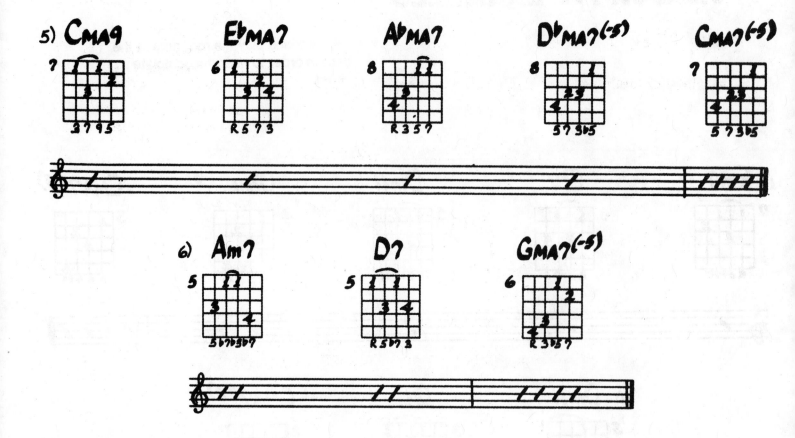

5) Cma9   E♭ma7   A♭ma7   D♭ma7(-5)   Cma7(-5)

6) Am7   D7   Gma7(-5)

● MAJOR 7 + 5

● Keyboard Analysis:

●● Used most often in a deceptive cadence or as an ending chord.

CHORD FORMS

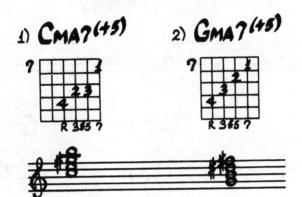

●

● MAJOR 7 + 5 EXAMPLES

● ● Have a friend play the root note in the bass in order to hear the complete chord.

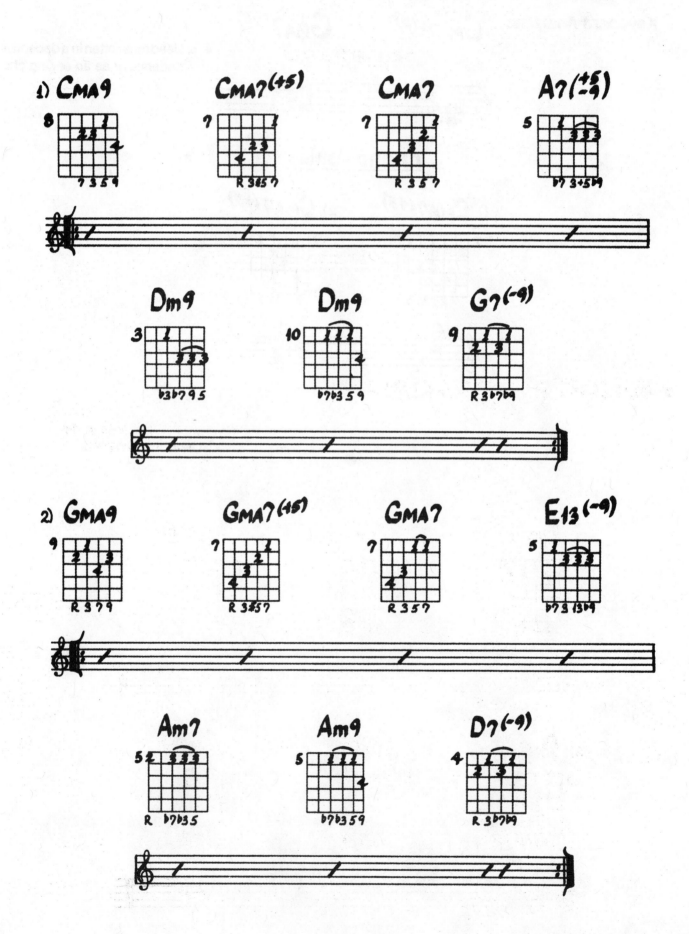

● MAJOR 9♭5

● **Keyboard Analysis:**

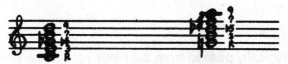

● ● Used most often as an ending chord.

CHORD FORMS

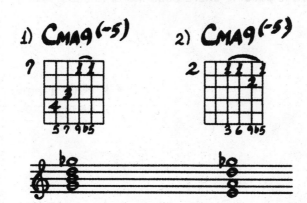

● MAJOR 9♭5 EXAMPLES

● ● Have a friend play the root note in the bass in order to hear the complete chord.

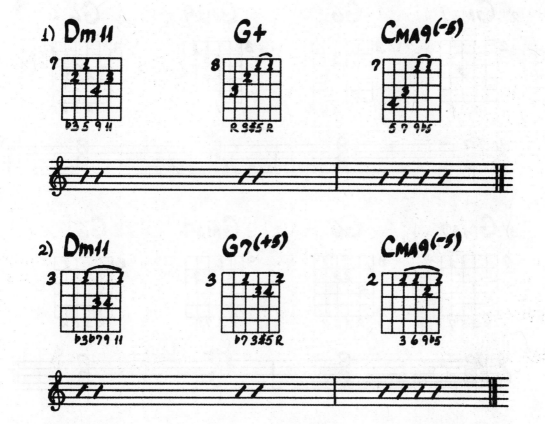

●PASSING MAJOR CHORDS (Ascending)

Major chords are typically passed from the ninth, root or the fifth of the chord. An ascending passing major chord will be passed from the fifth of the chord up. A descending passing major chord will be passed from the ninth or root of the chord down. Use the passing chord sequences to substitute for a single chord.

● ● Have a friend play the root note in the bass in order to hear the complete chord.

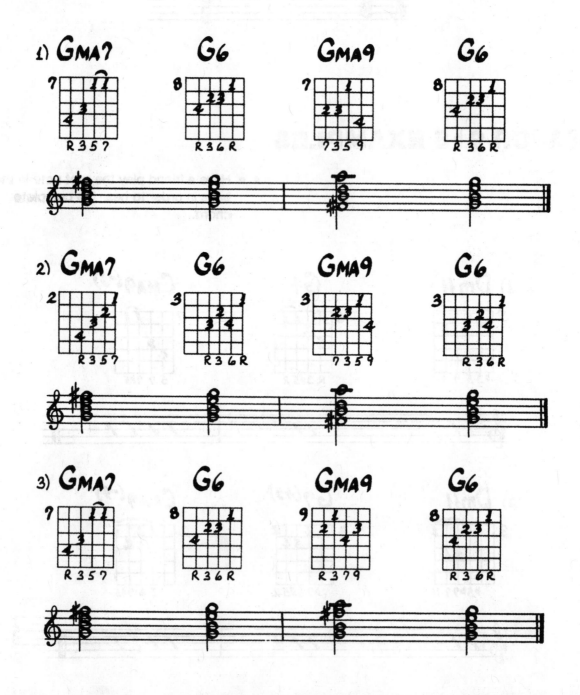

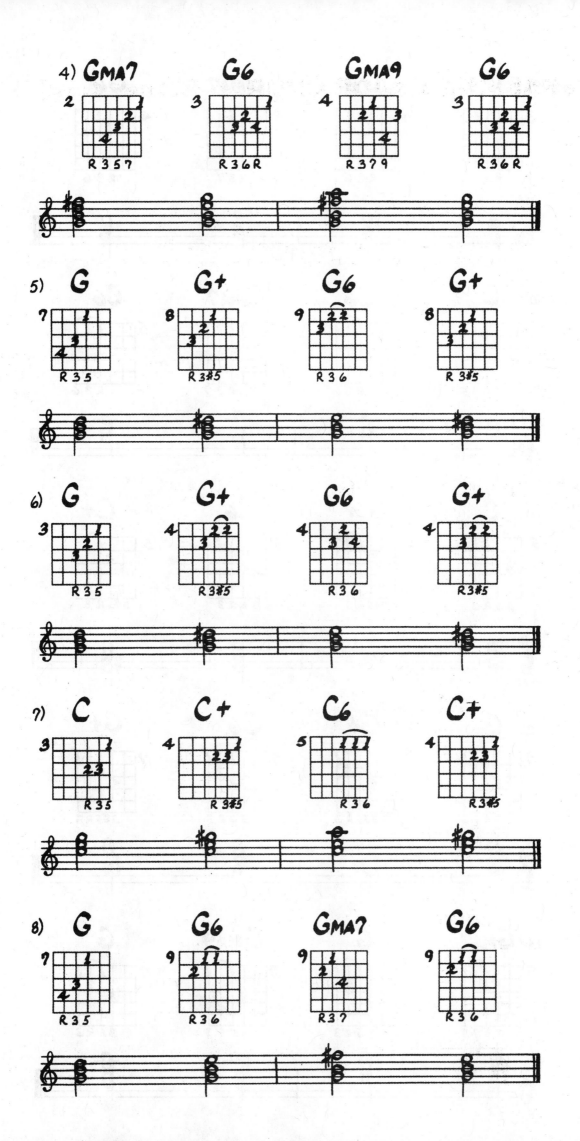

38

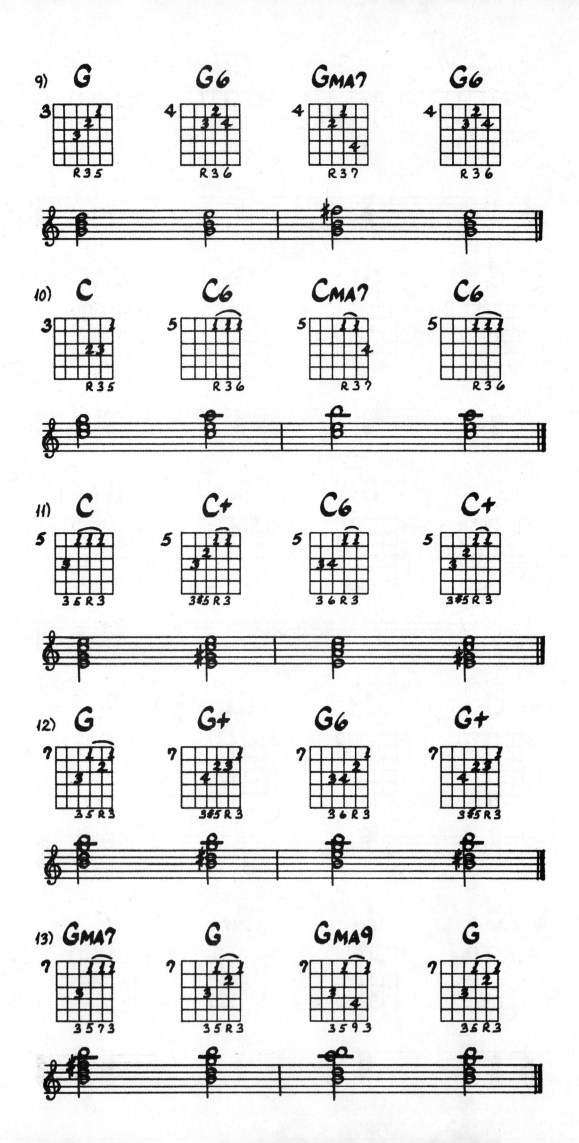

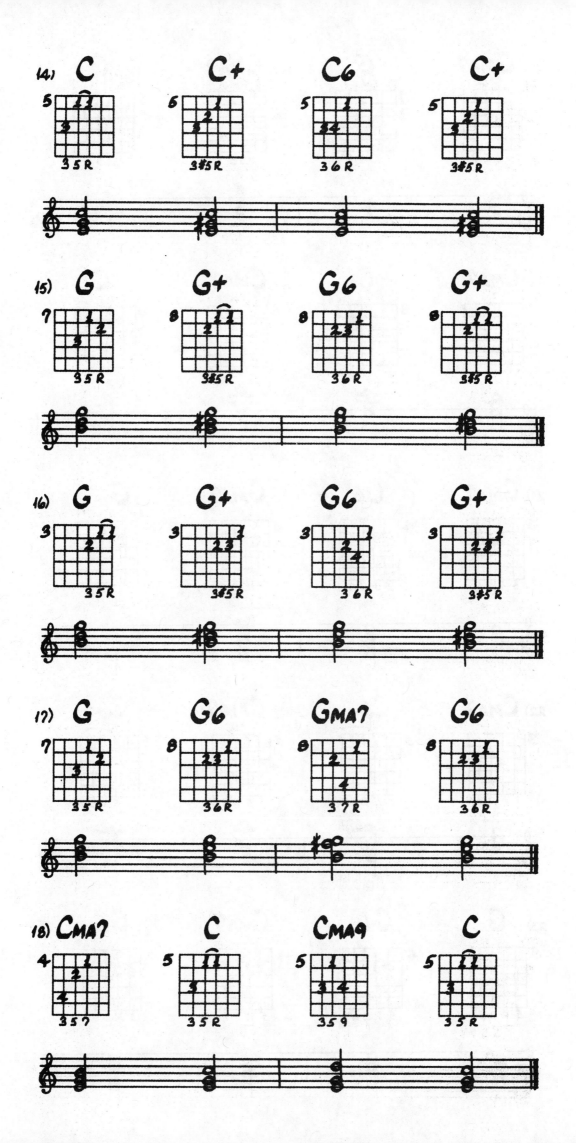

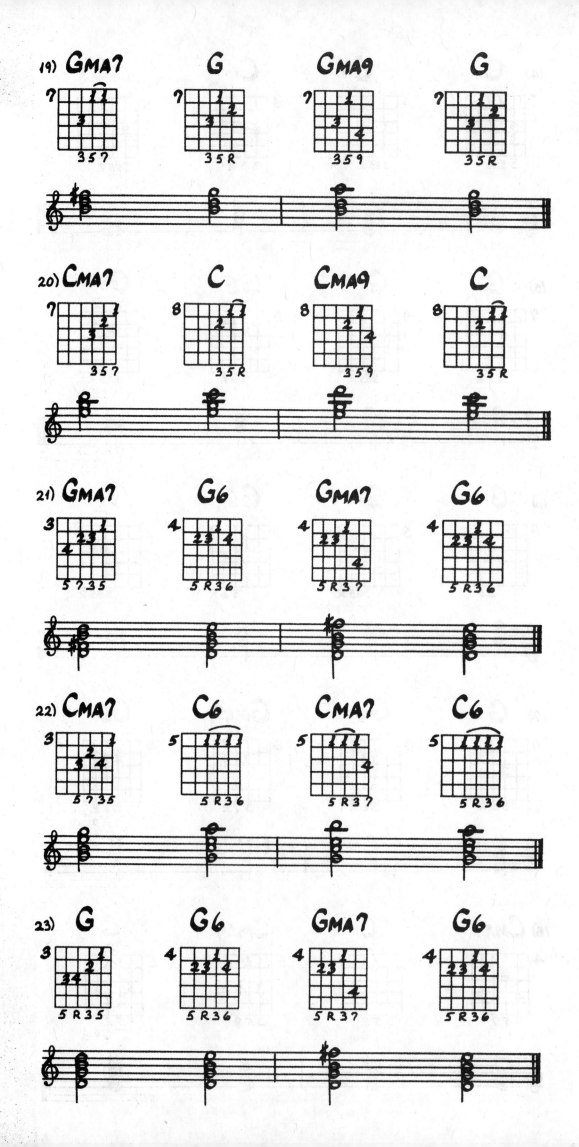

41

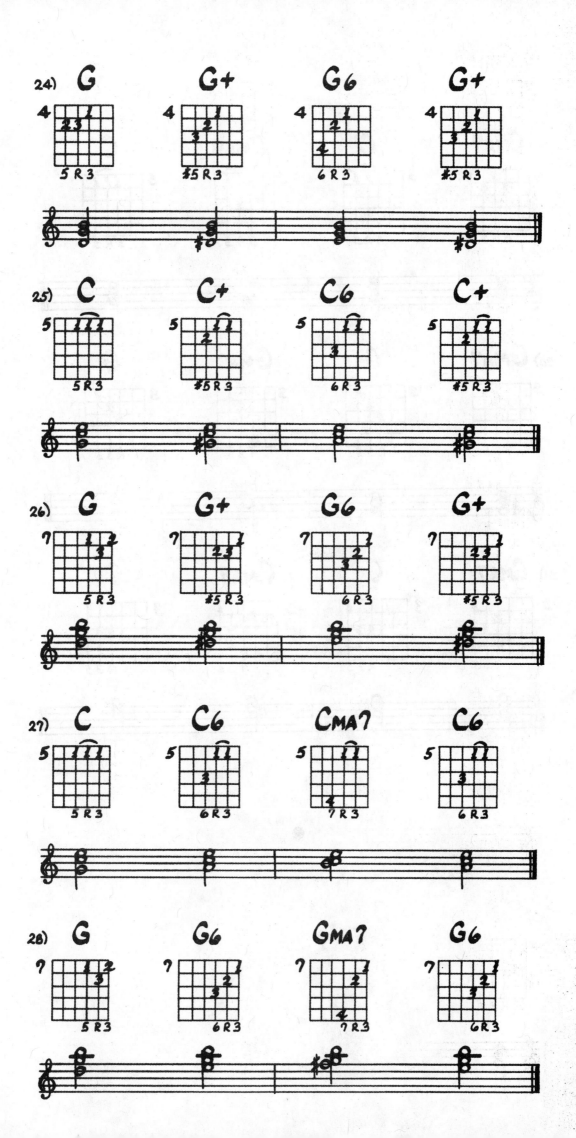

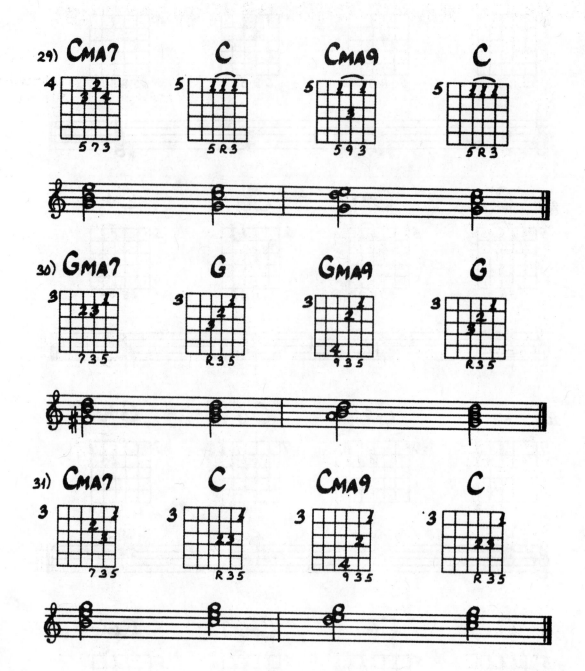

• PASSING MAJOR CHORDS (Descending)

• • Have a friend play the root note in the bass in order to hear the complete chord.

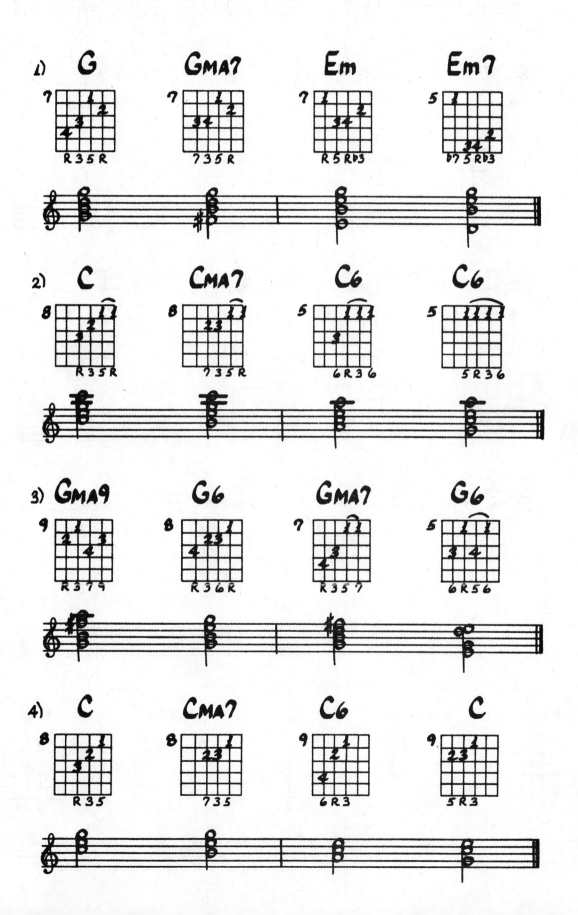

44

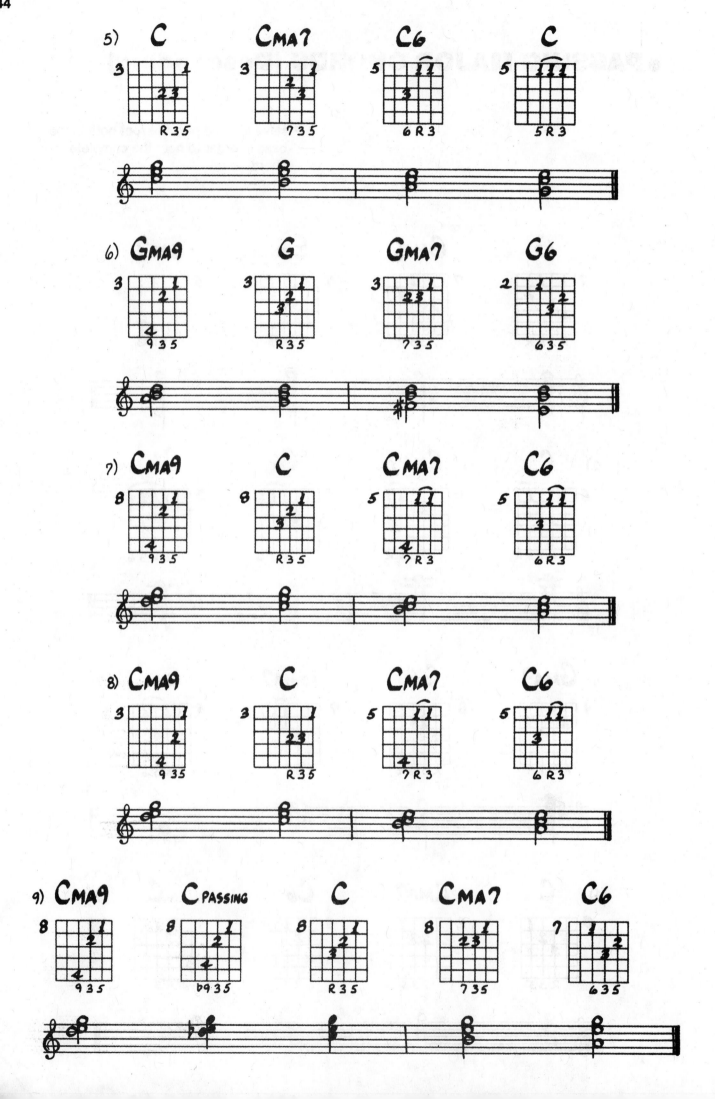

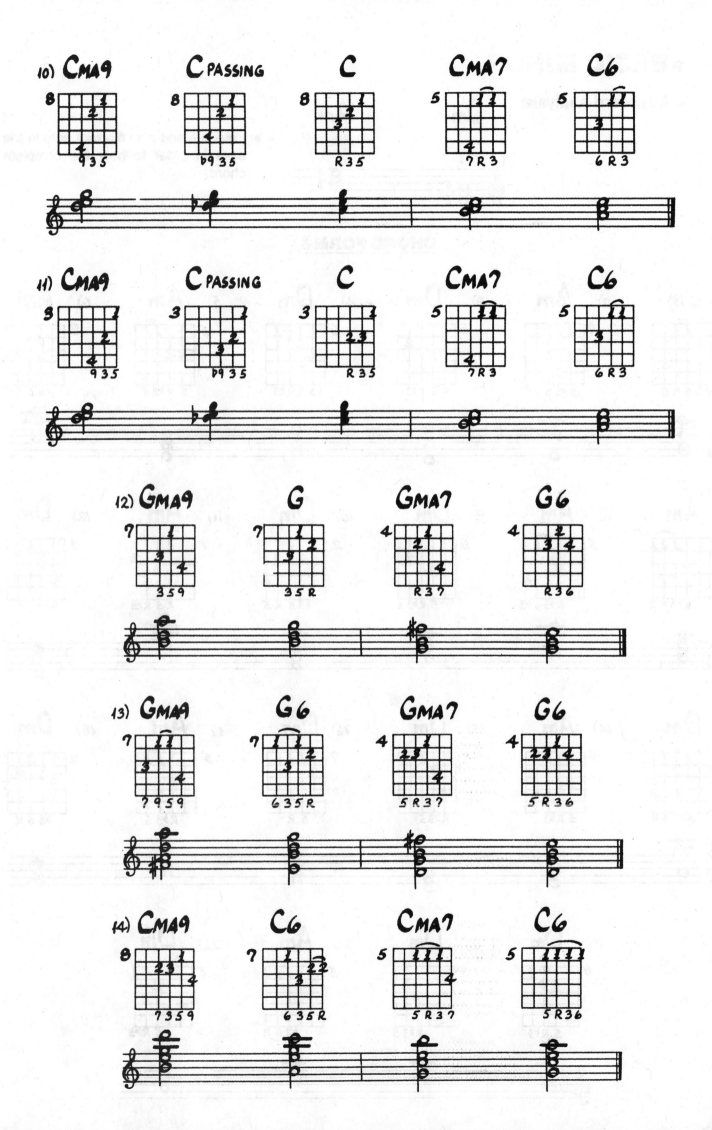

● BASIC MINOR

● Keyboard Analysis:

● ● Have a friend play the root note in the bass in order to hear the complete chord.

CHORD FORMS

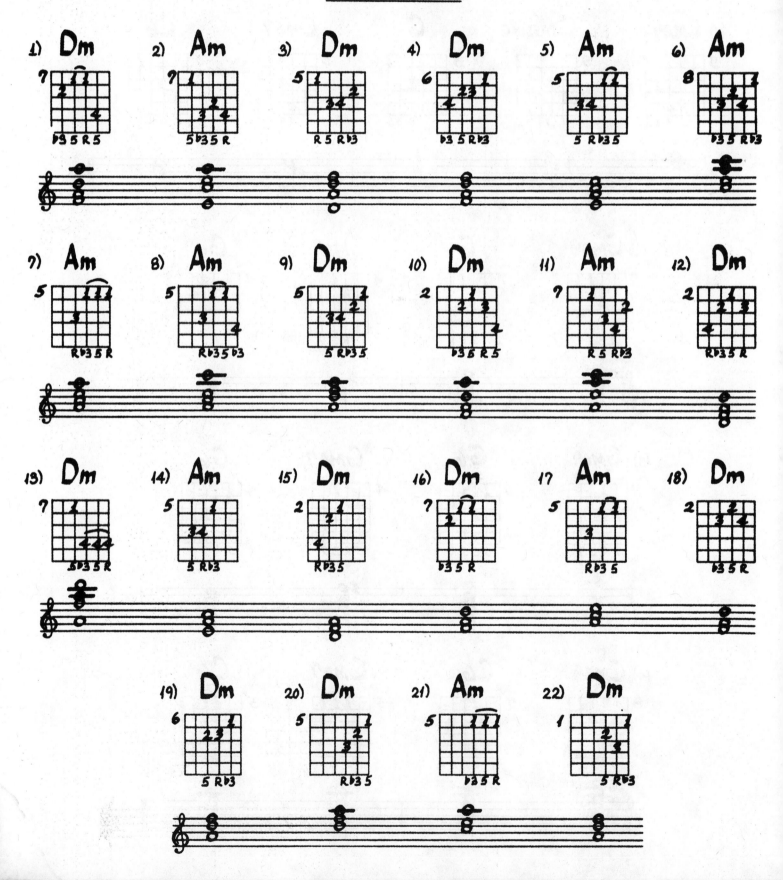

●BASIC MINOR EXAMPLES

● ● Have a friend play the root note in the bass in order to hear the complete chord.

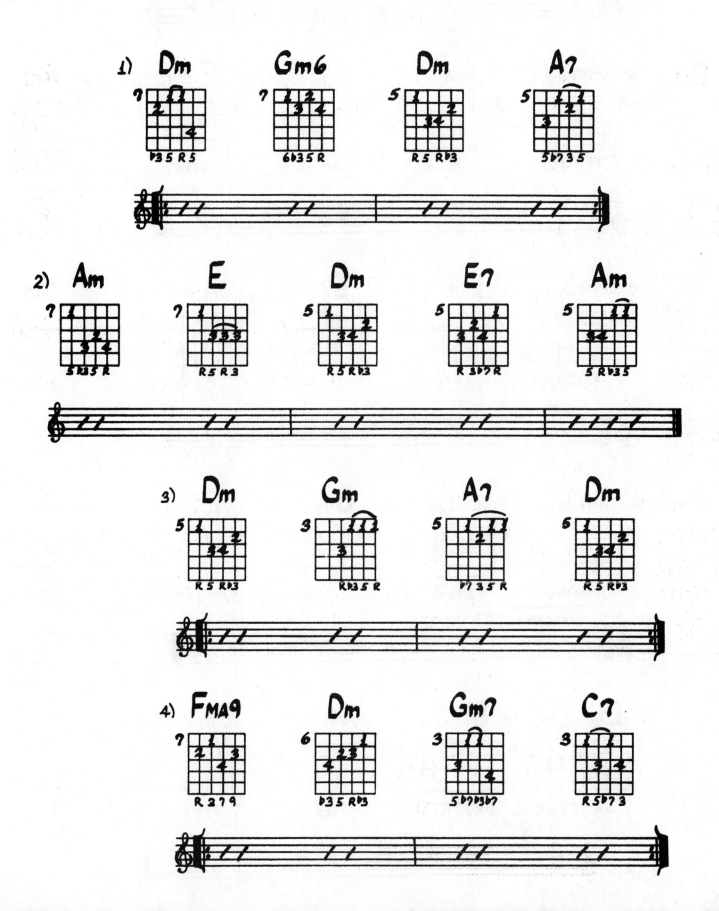

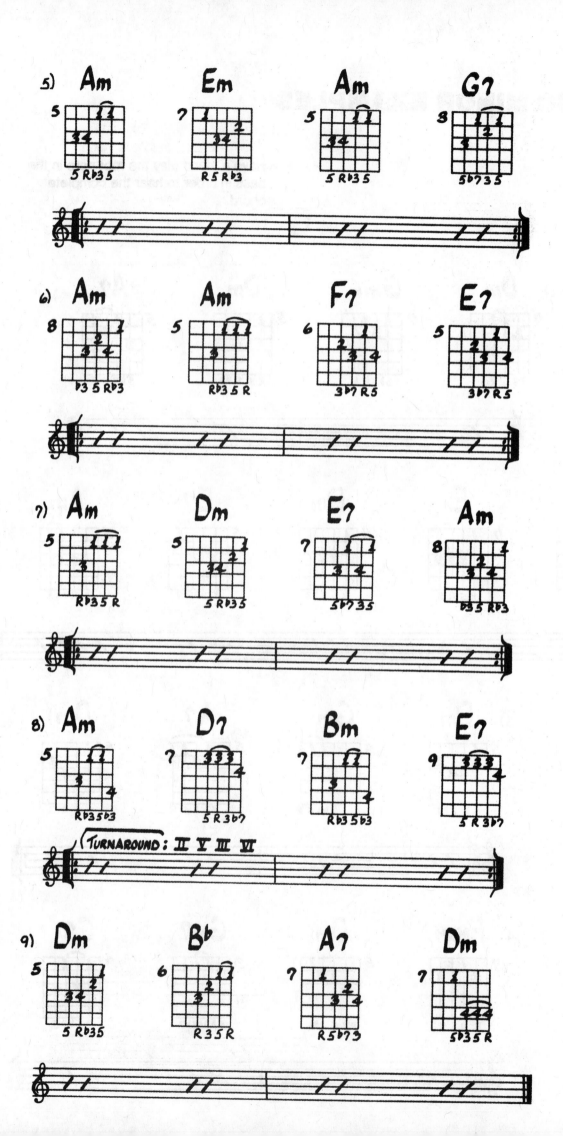

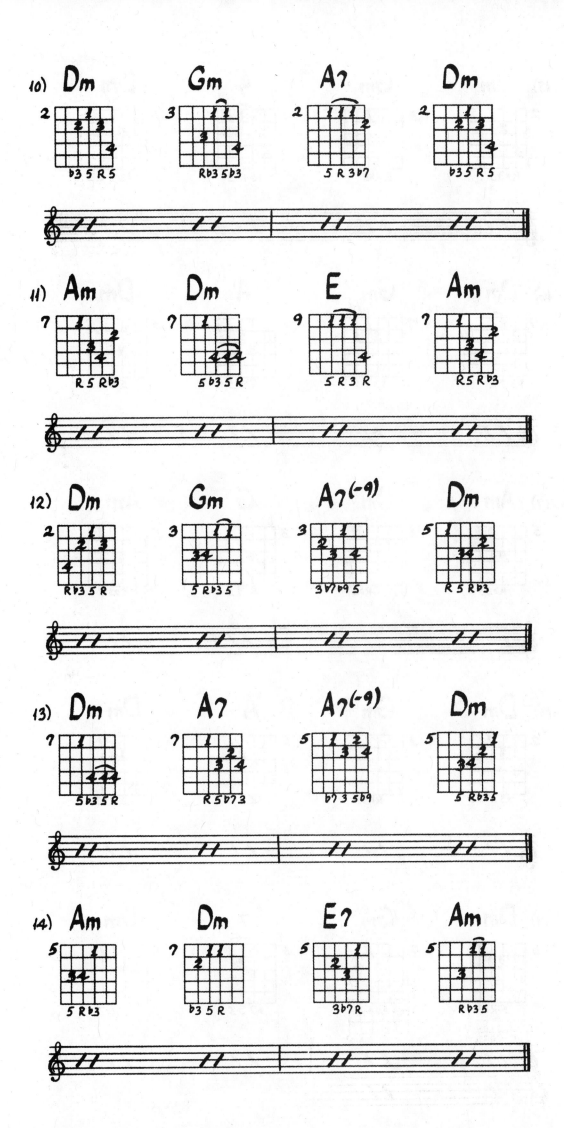

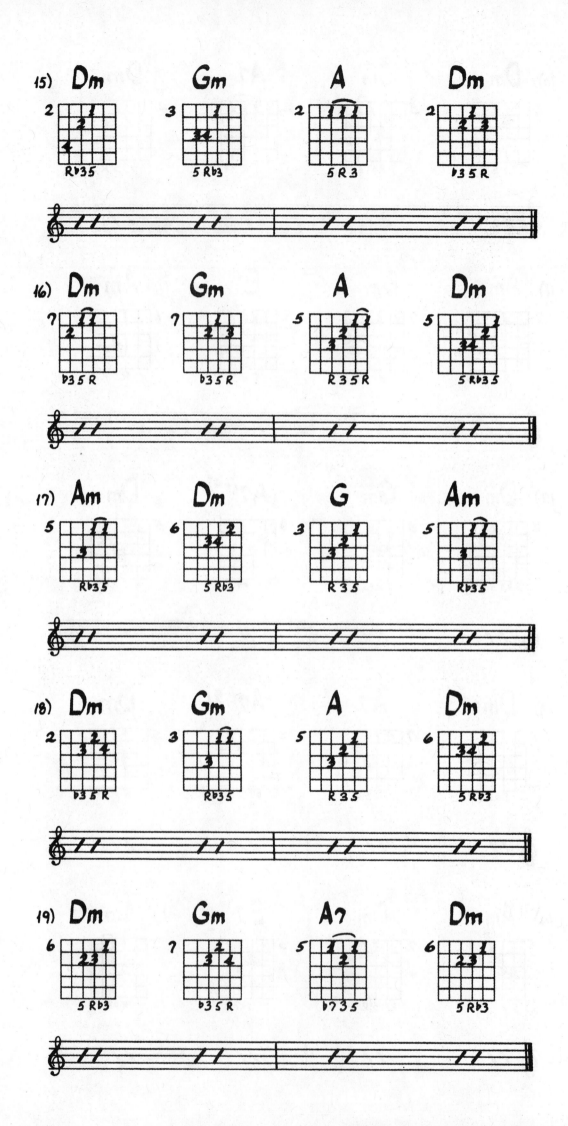

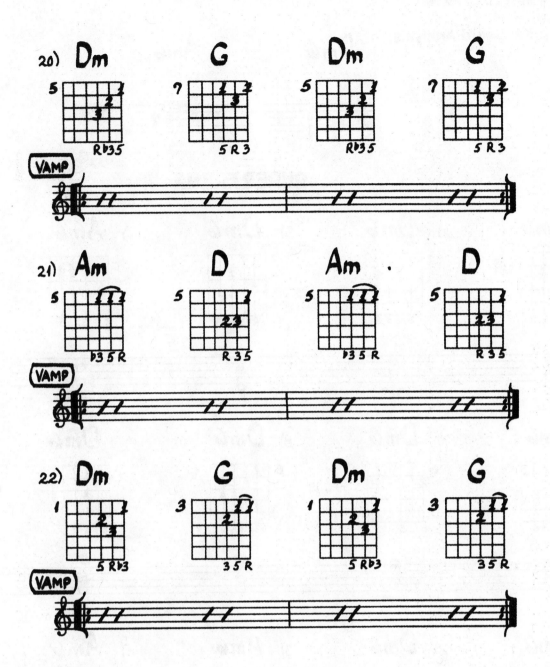

● MINOR 6

● Keyboard Analysis:

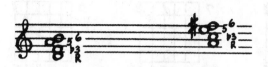

CHORD FORMS

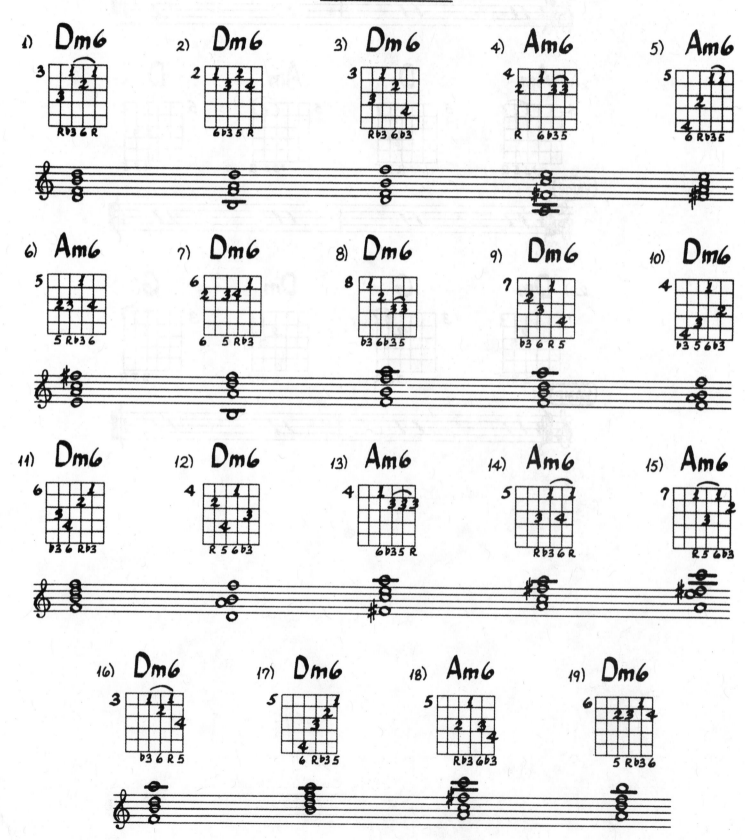

● MINOR 6 EXAMPLES

● ● Have a friend play the root note in the bass in order to hear the complete chord.

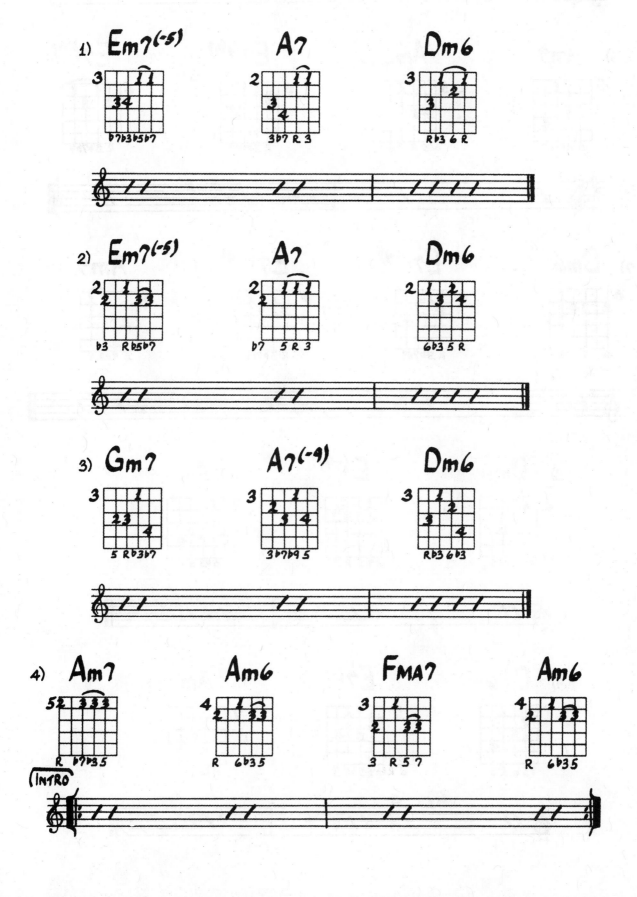

54

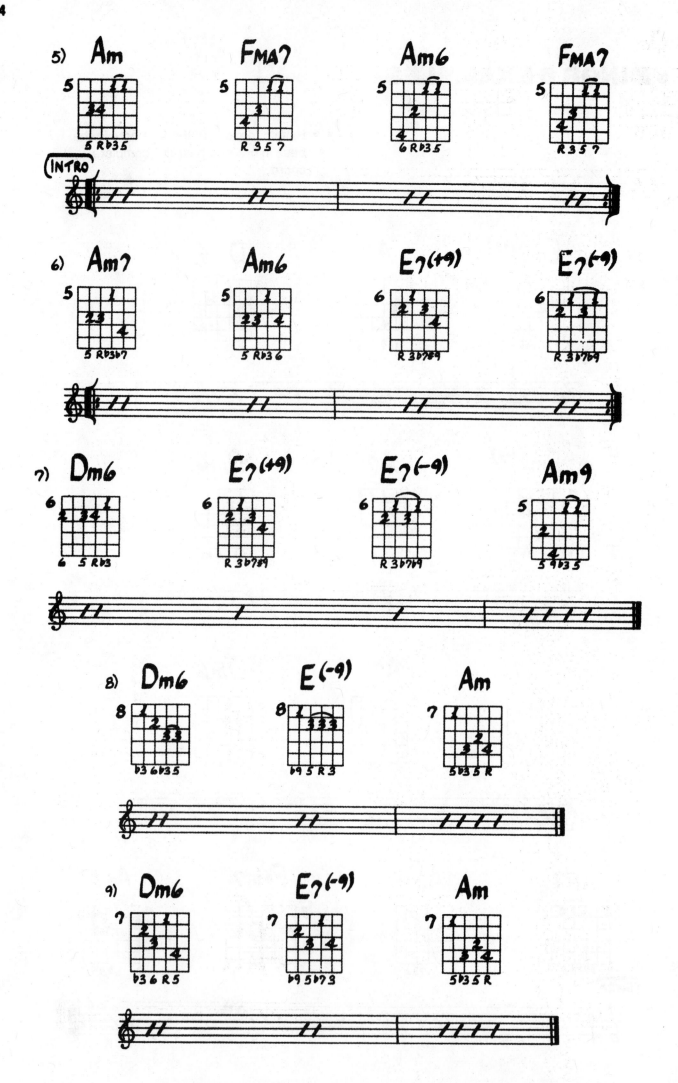

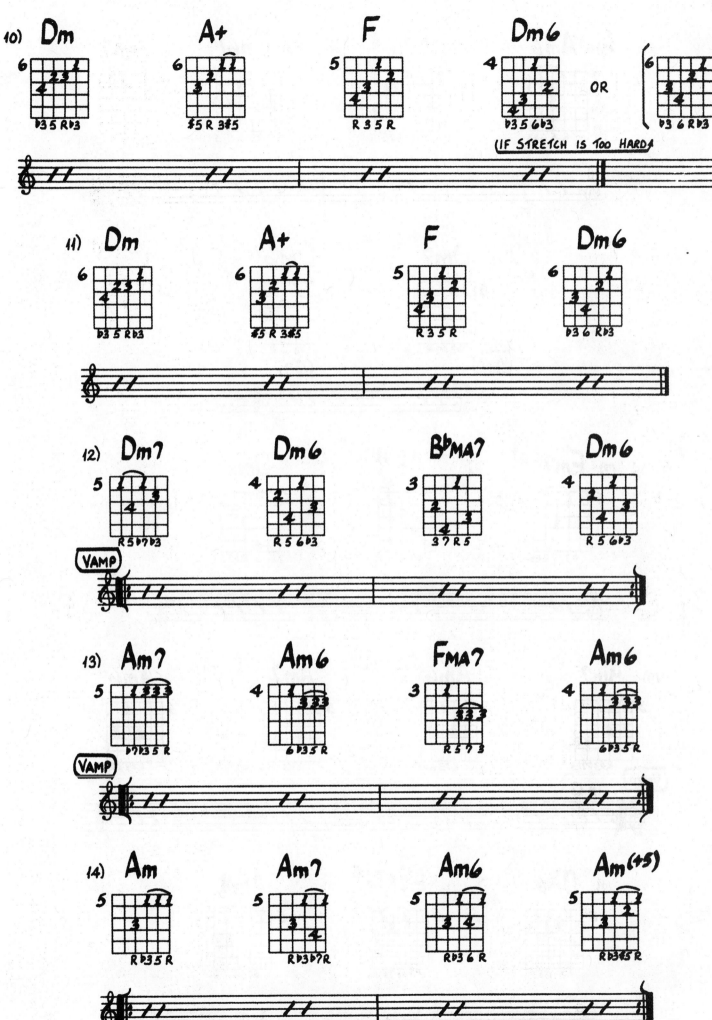

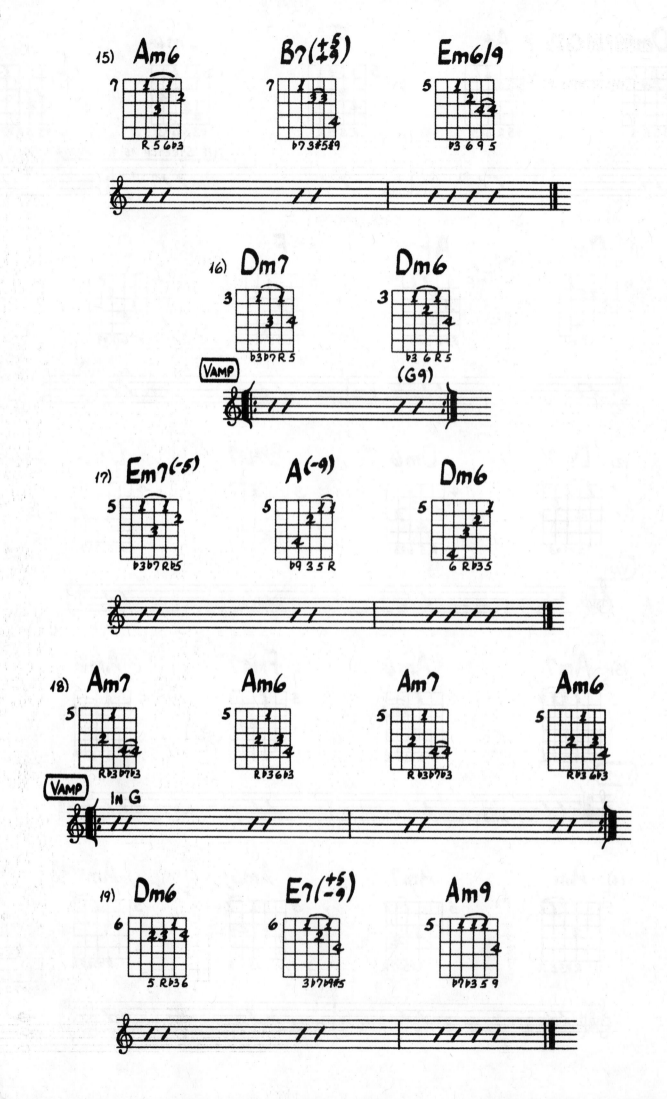

● MINOR 7

● **Keyboard Analysis:**

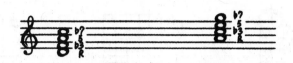

CHORD FORMS

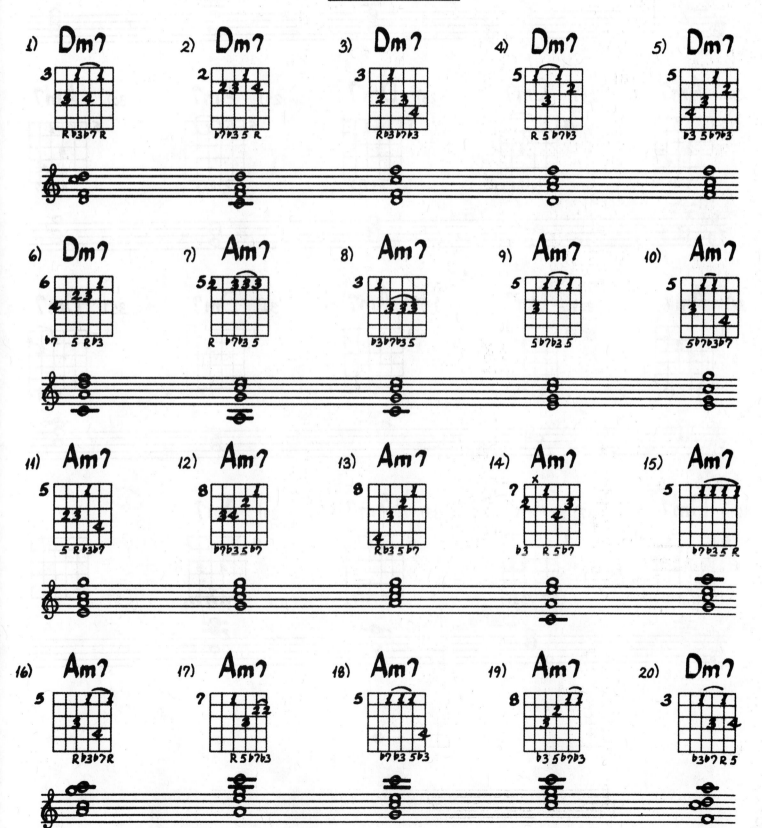

58

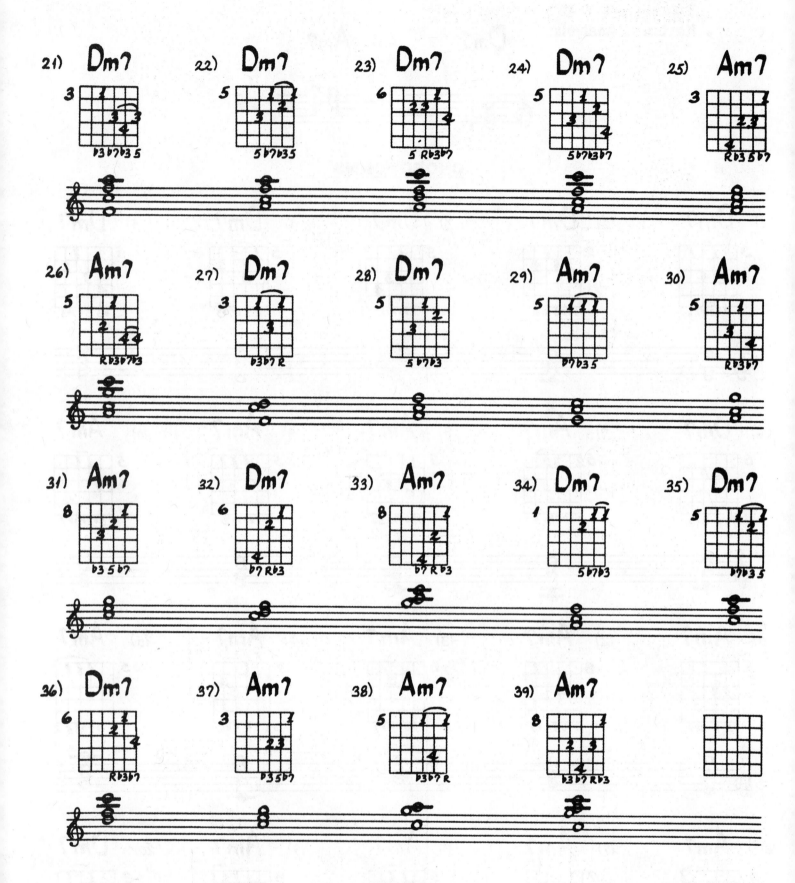

●MINOR 7 EXAMPLES

● ● Have a friend play the root note in the bass in order to hear the complete chord.

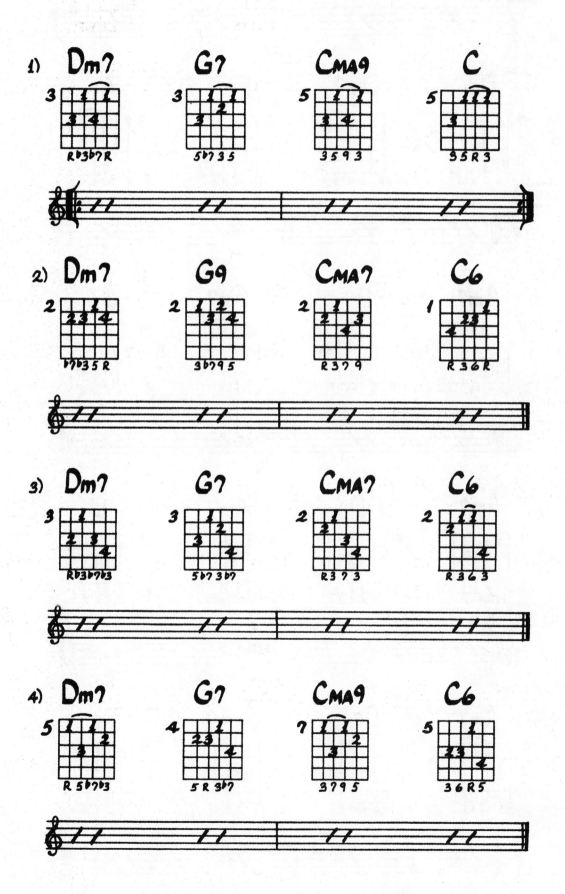

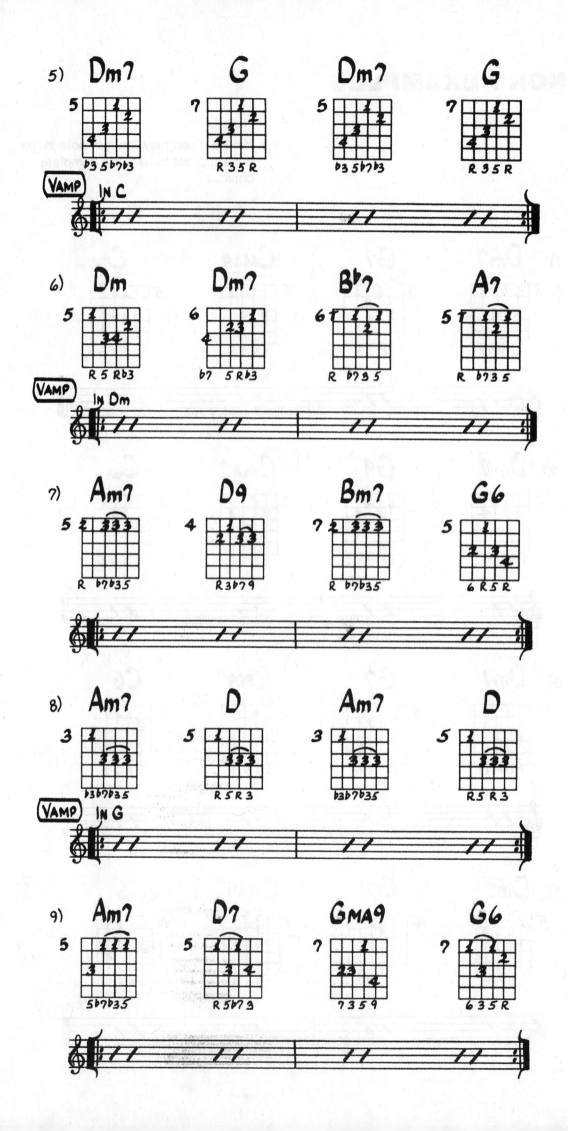

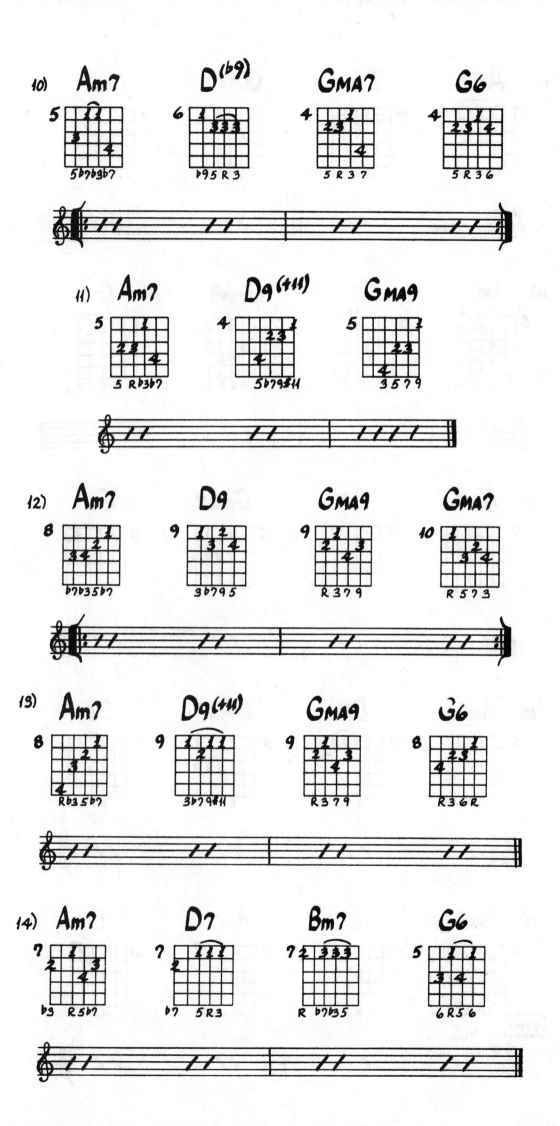

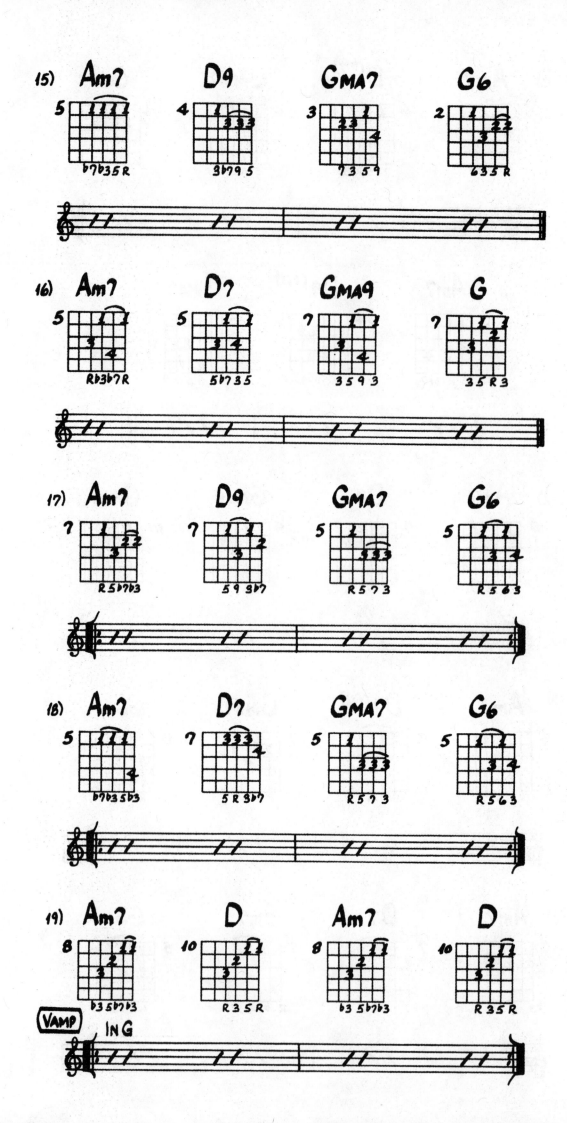

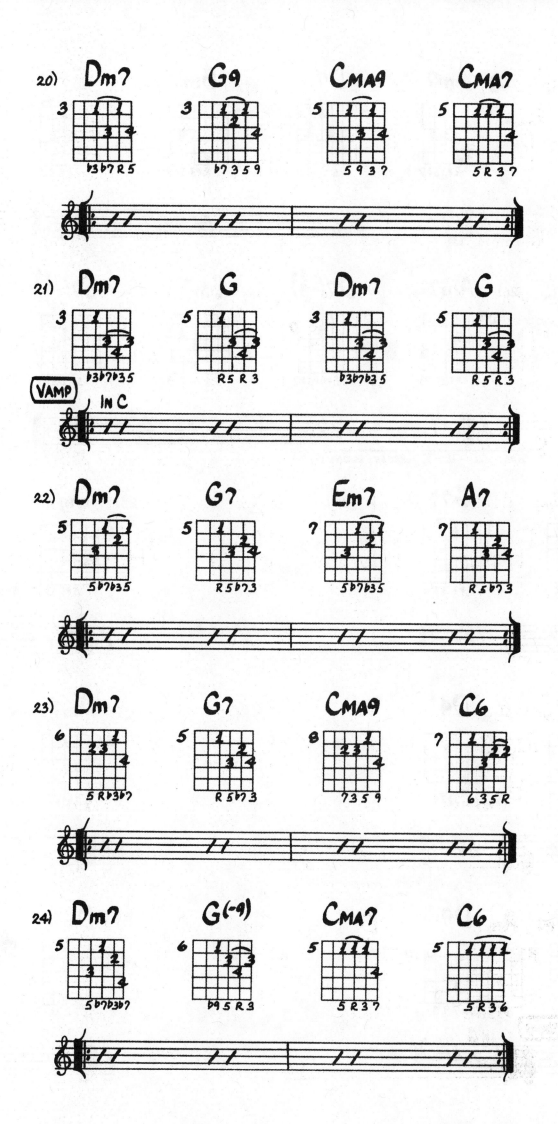

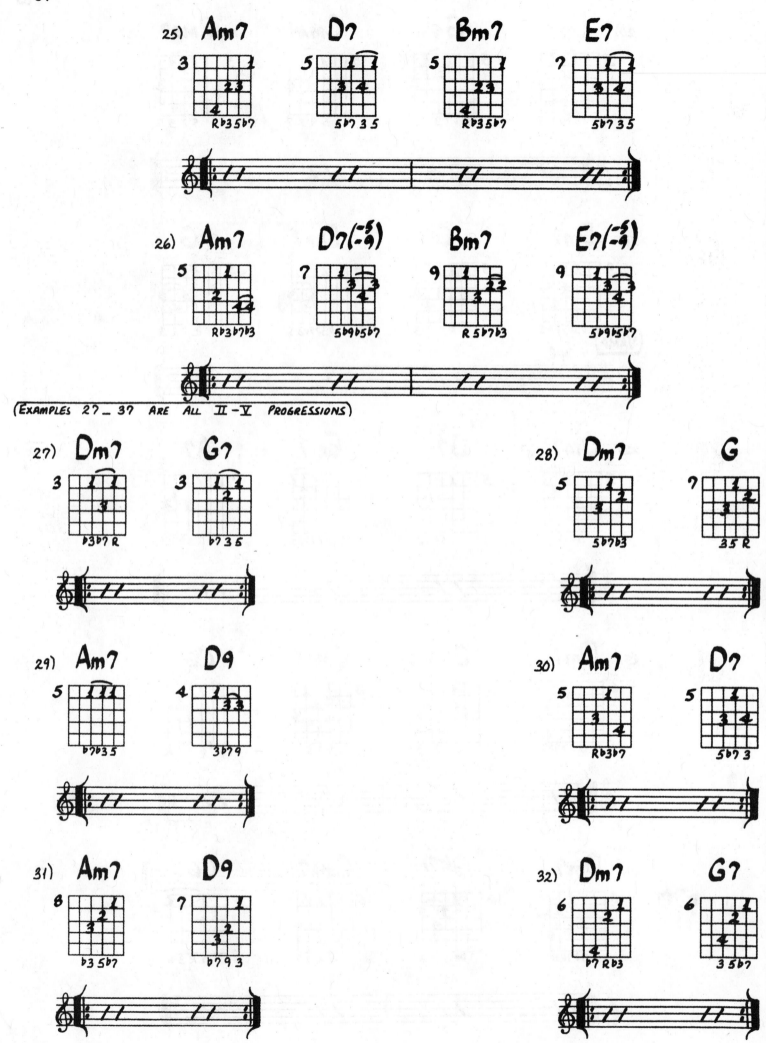

(EXAMPLES 27 — 37 ARE ALL II – V PROGRESSIONS)

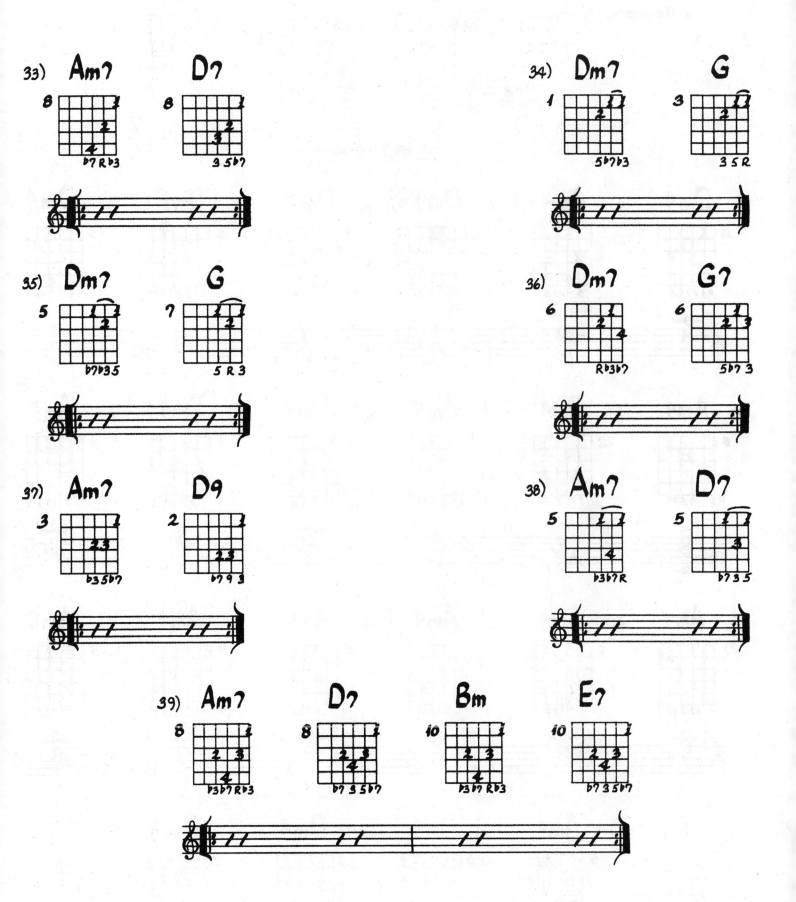

● MINOR 9

● **Keyboard Analysis:**

CHORD FORMS

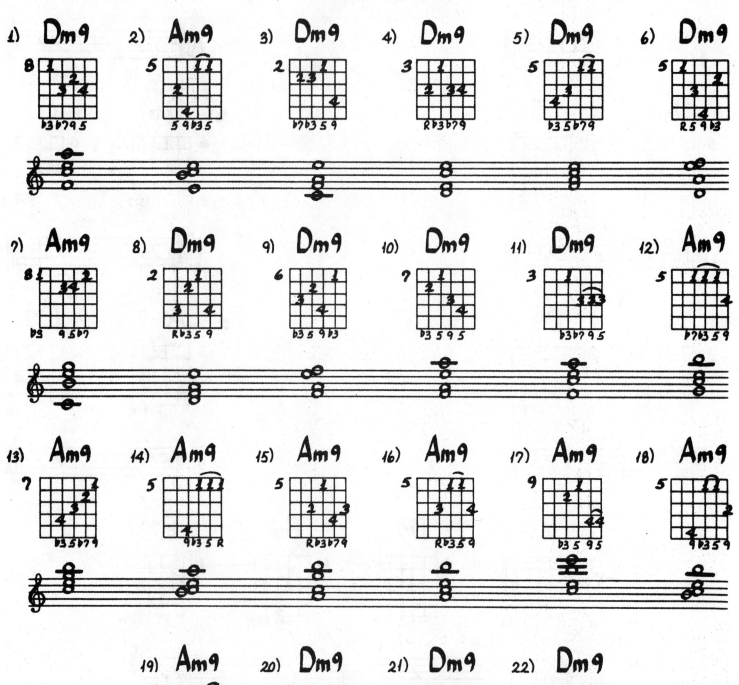

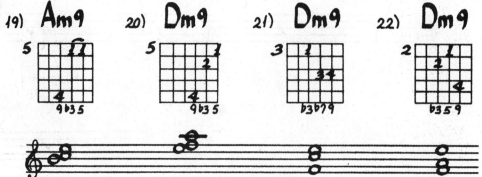

●MINOR 9 EXAMPLES

● ● Have a friend play the root note in the bass in order to hear the complete chord.

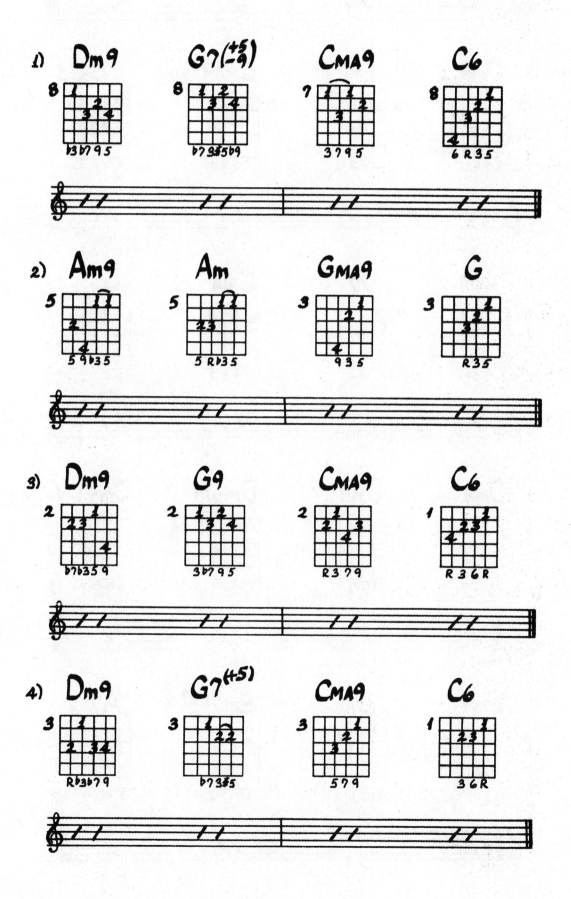

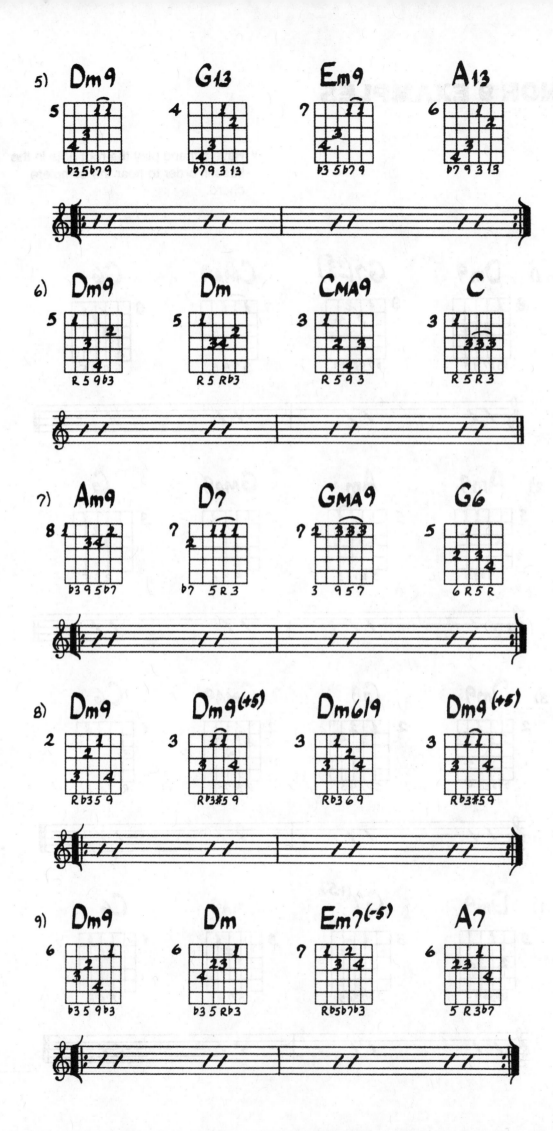

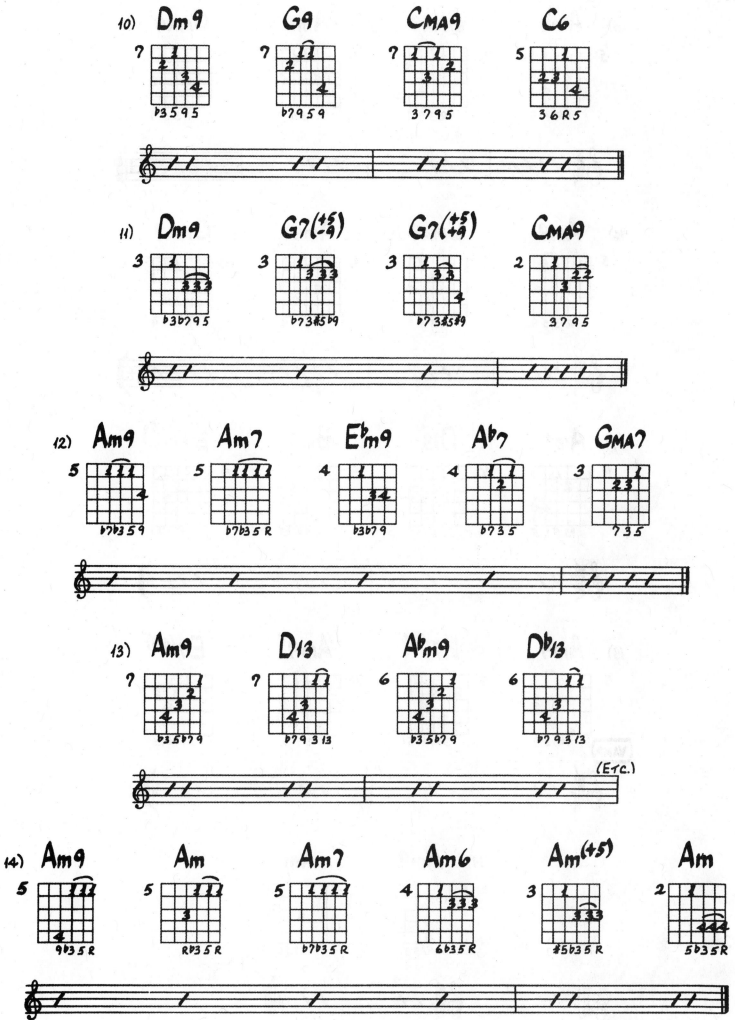

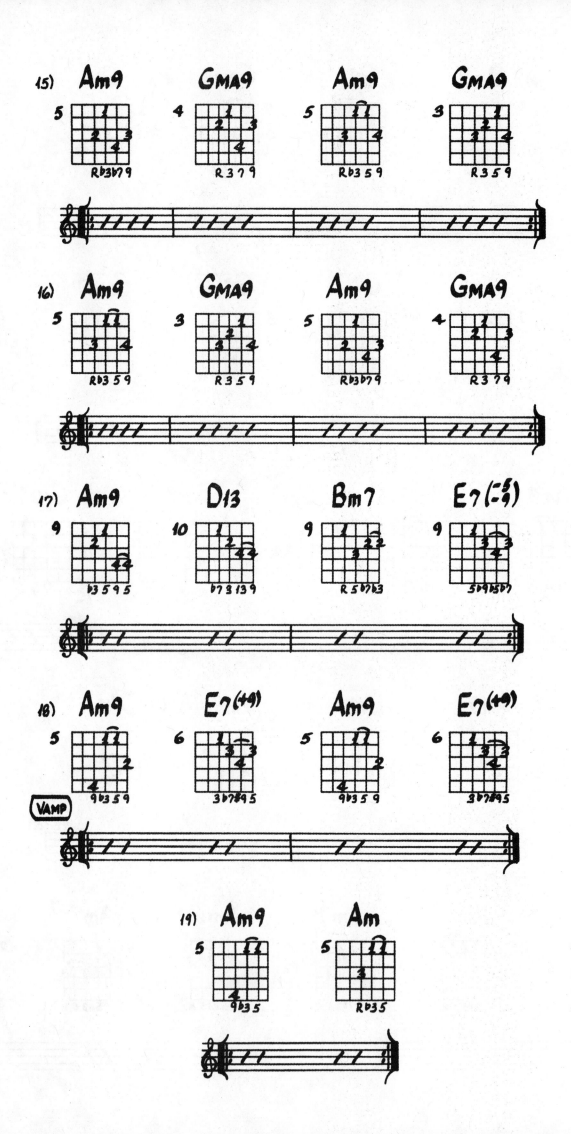

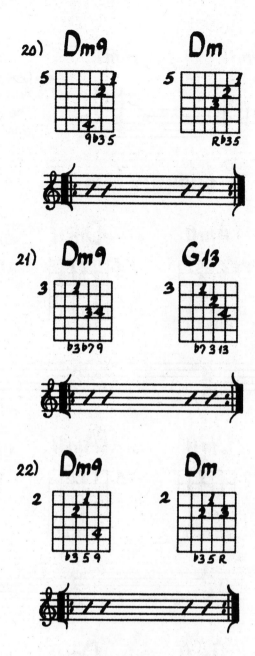

●MINOR 11

● **Keyboard Analysis:**

● ●Dm11 can usually be called G11 or G7sus. Am11 can usually be called D11 or D7sus. The exceptions here are Chords 2, 14, 20 which are not Dominant 11 chords.

CHORD FORMS

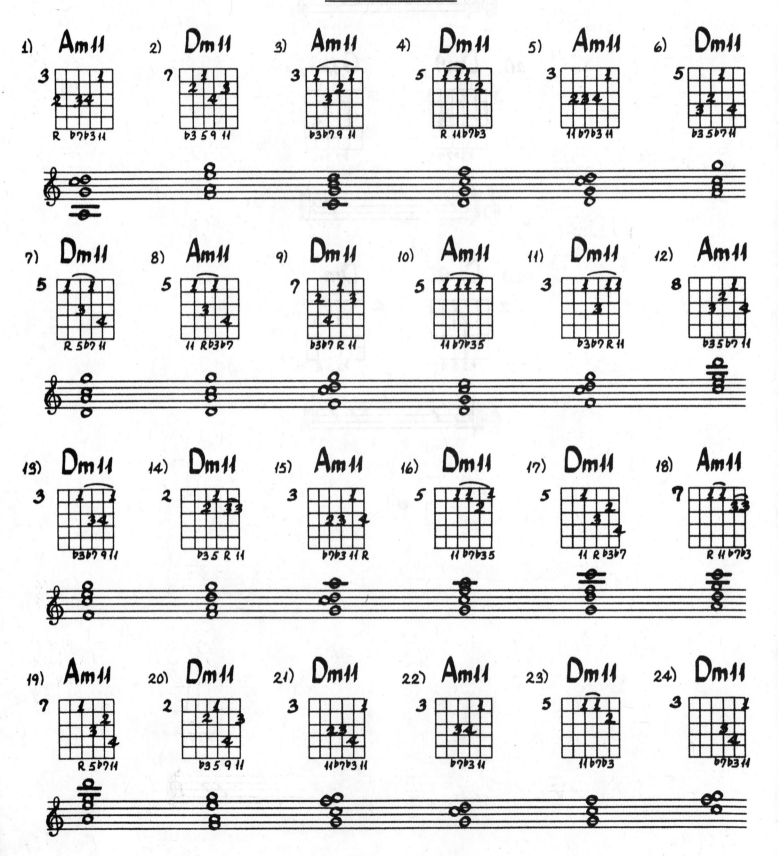

● MINOR 11 EXAMPLES

● ● Have a friend play the root note in the bass in order to hear the complete chord.

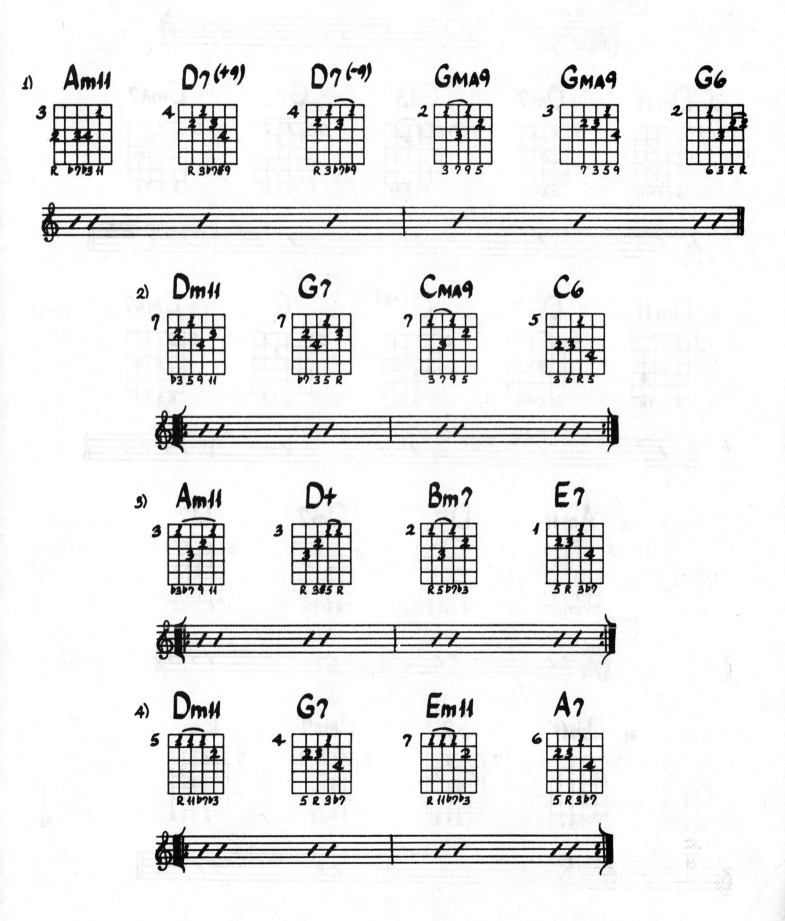

74

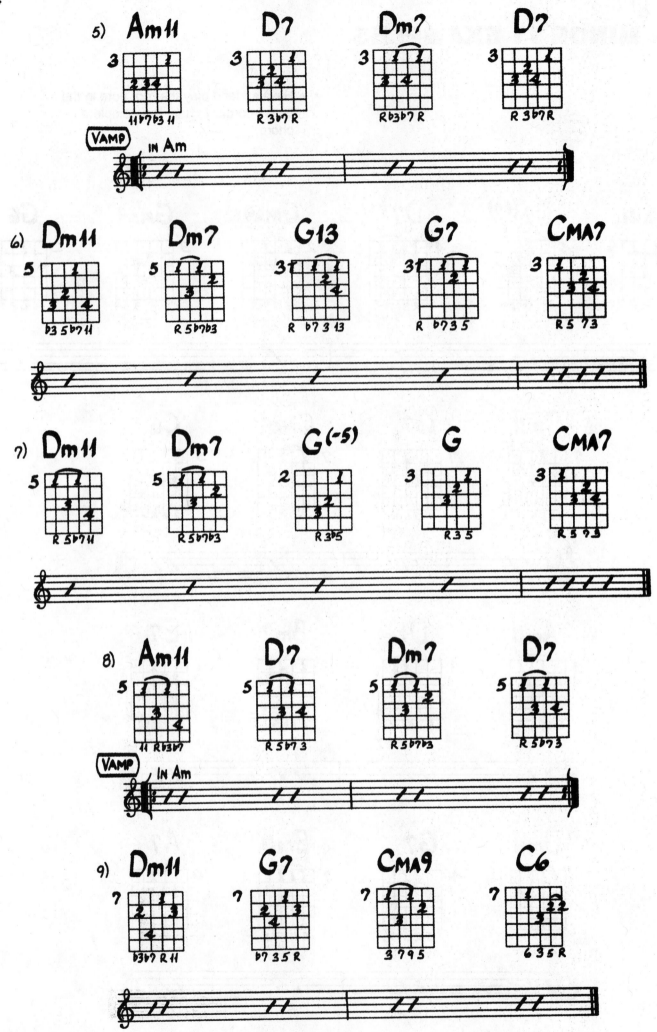

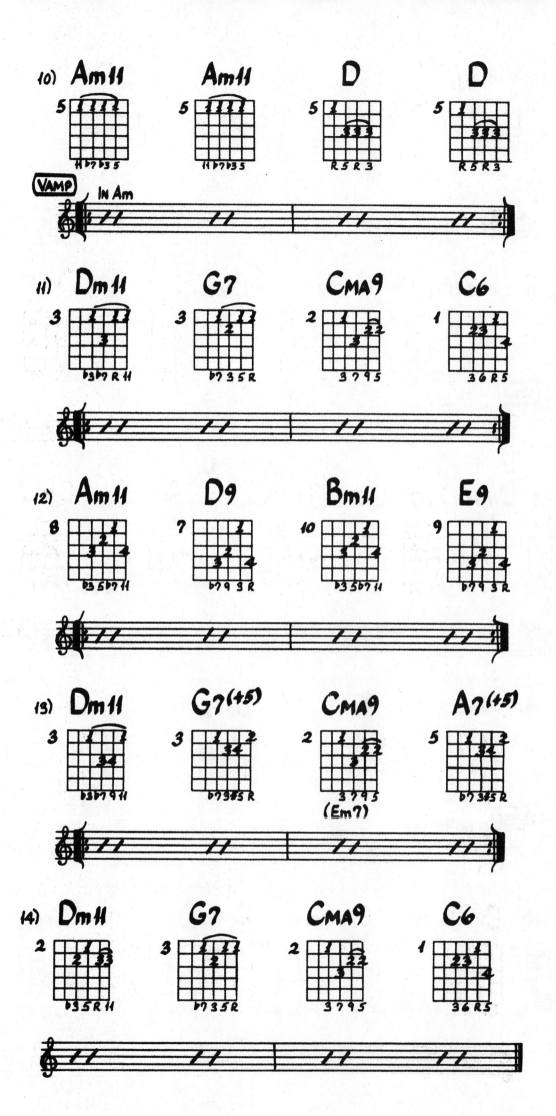

76

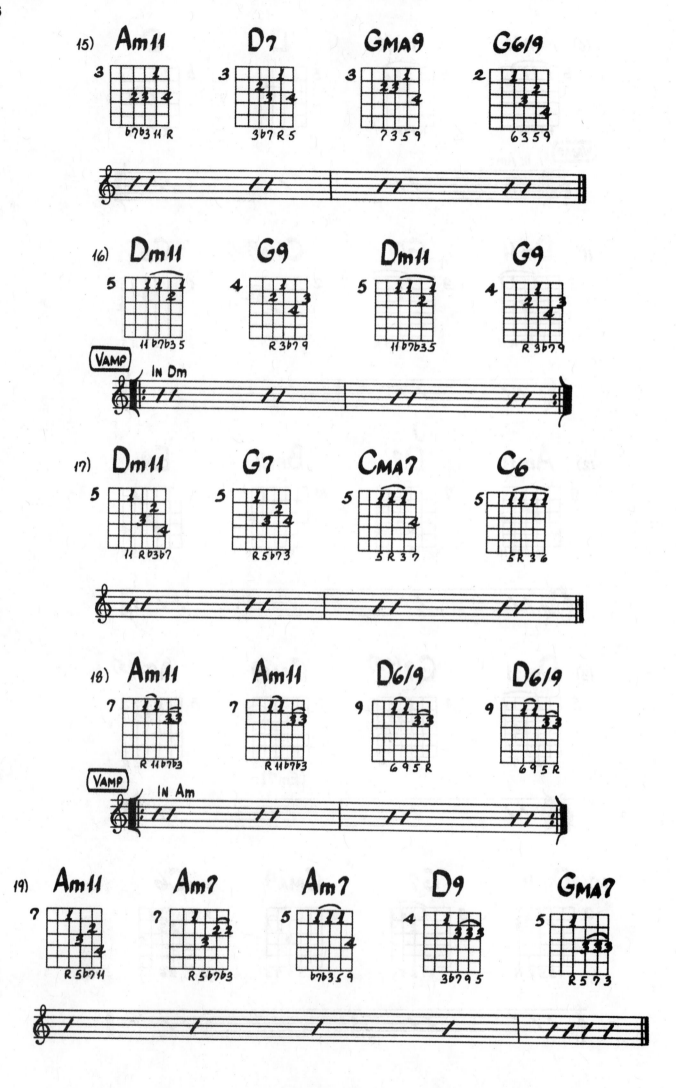

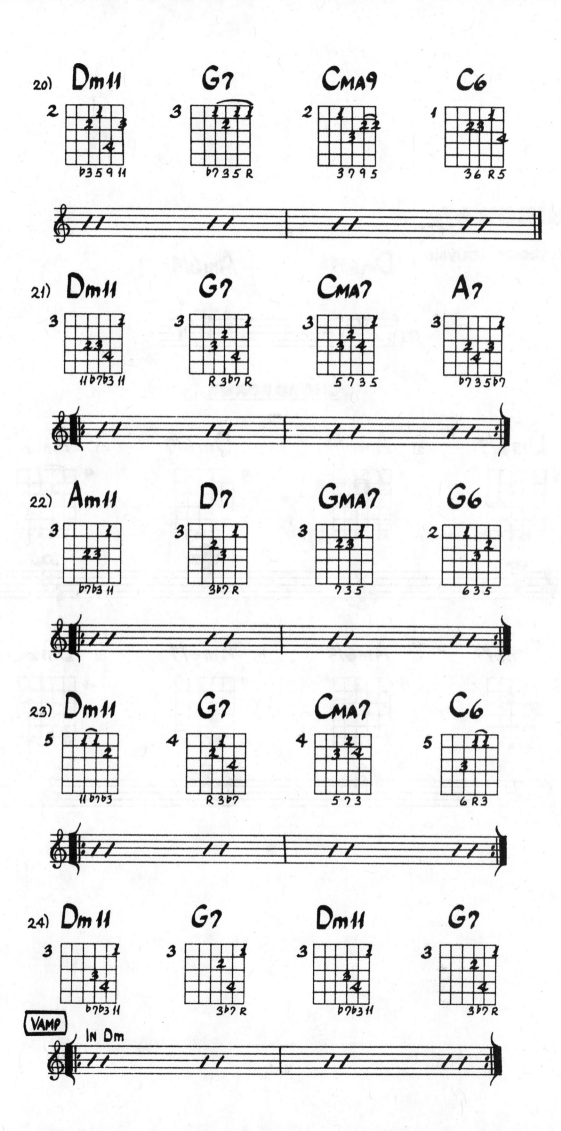

● MINOR 6/9

● Keyboard Analysis:

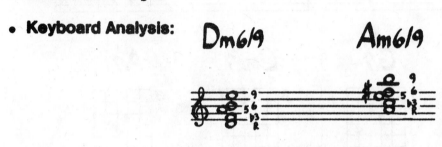

CHORD FORMS

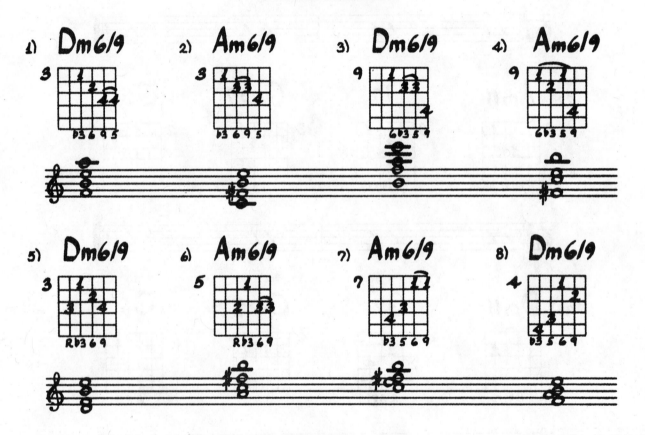

● MINOR 6/9 EXAMPLES

● ● Have a friend play the root note in the bass in order to hear the complete chord.

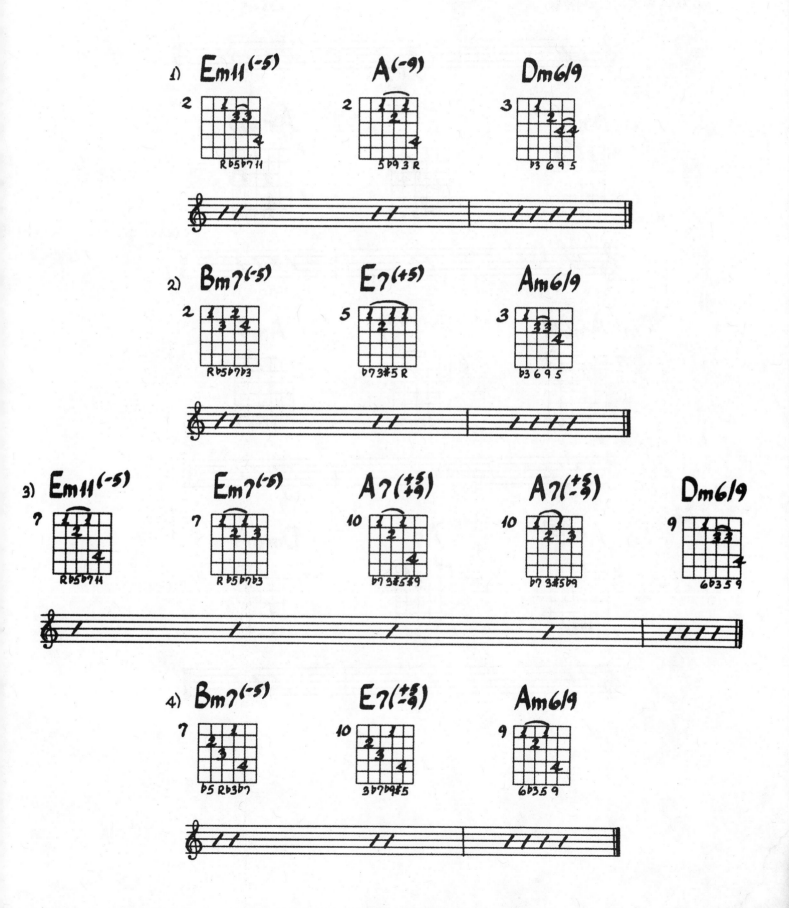

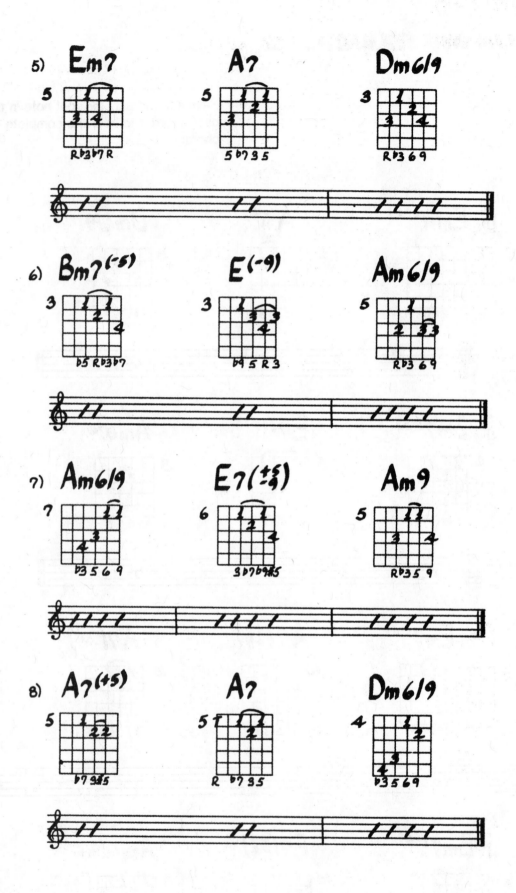

• MINOR 7♭5

- **Keyboard Analysis:**

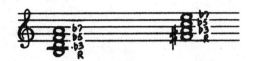

•• Many Minor 7♭5 forms are also used as Dom 9ths or Minor 6ths.

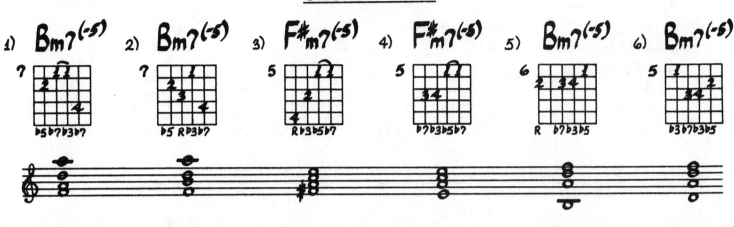

CHORD FORMS

   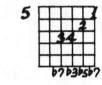 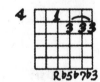 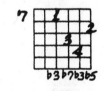

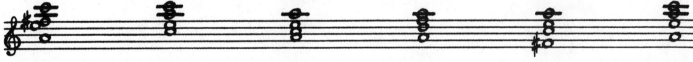

● MINOR 7♭5 EXAMPLES

●● Have a friend play the root note in the bass in order to hear the complete chord.

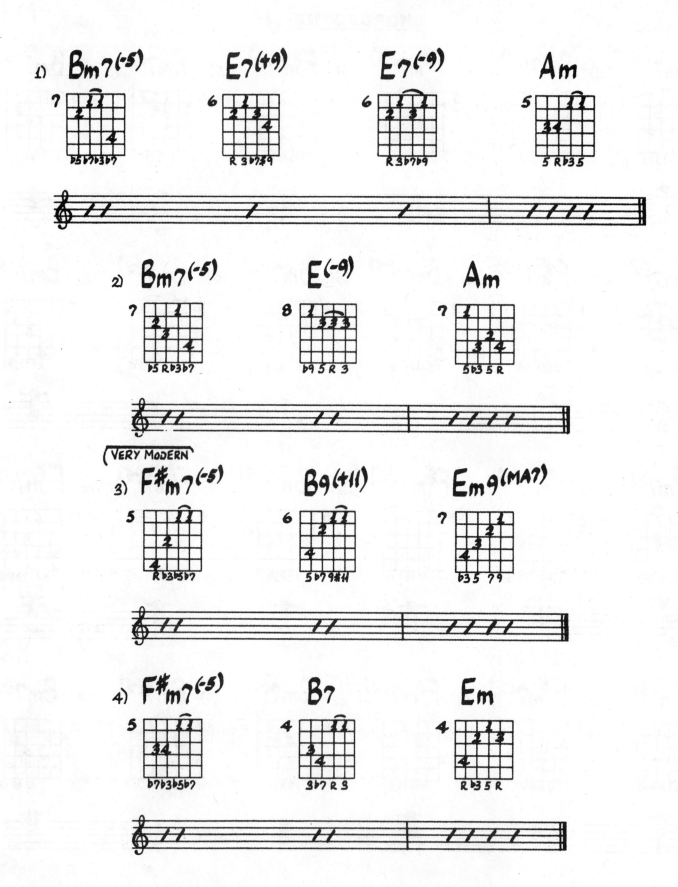

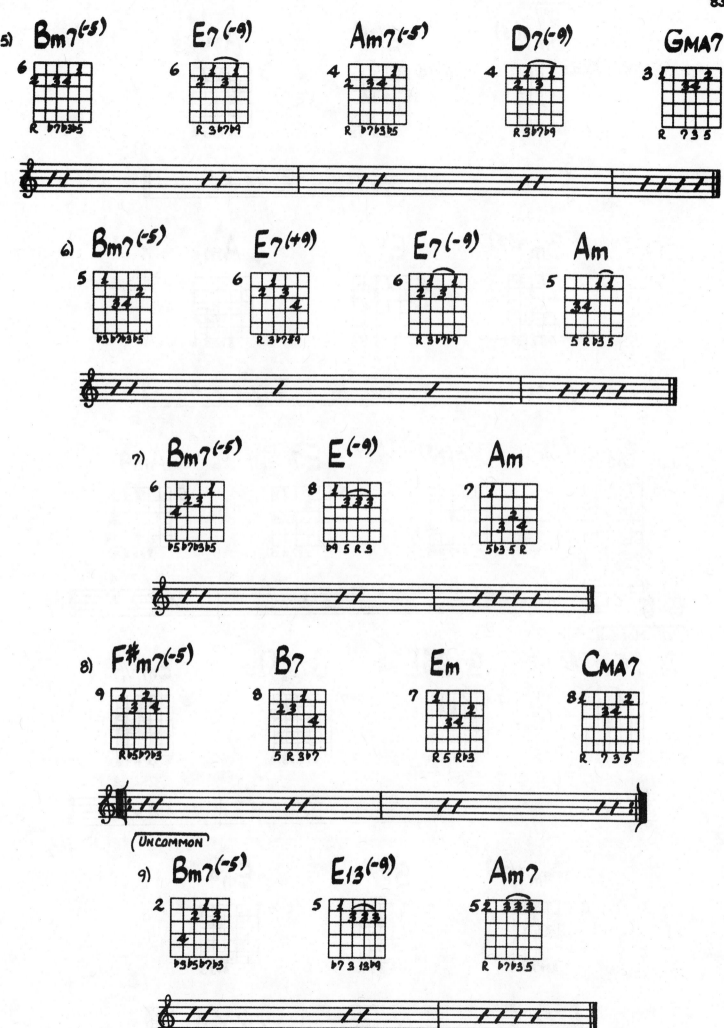

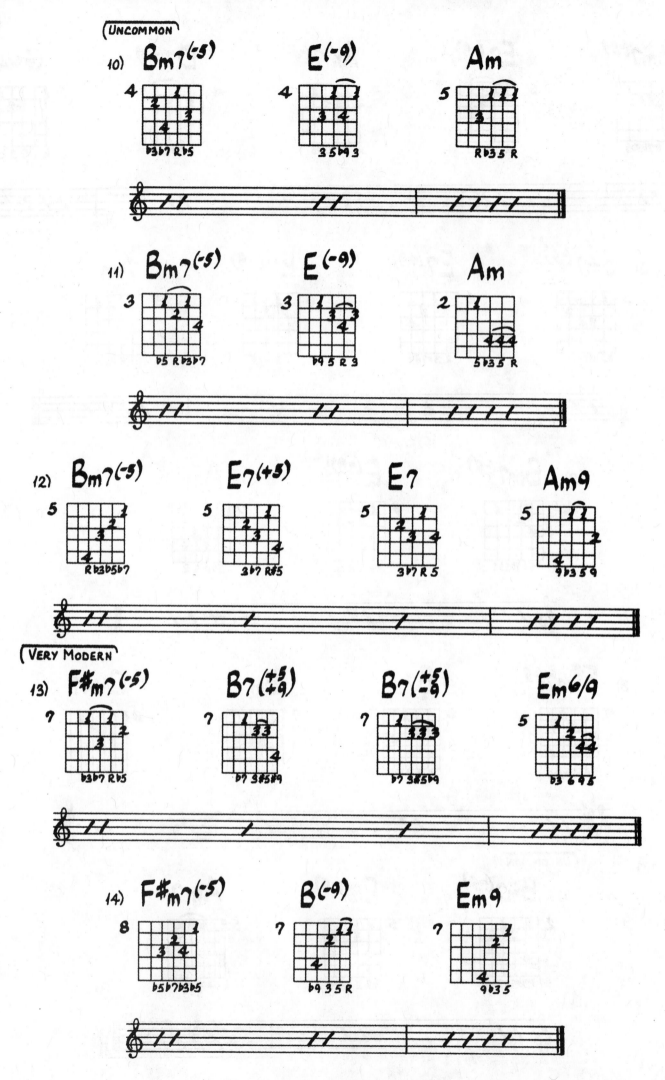

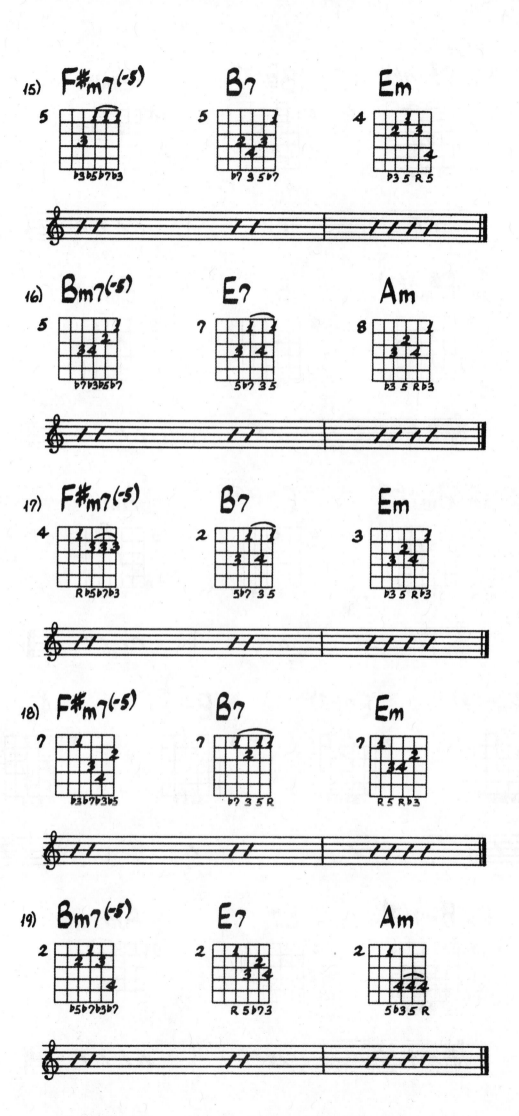

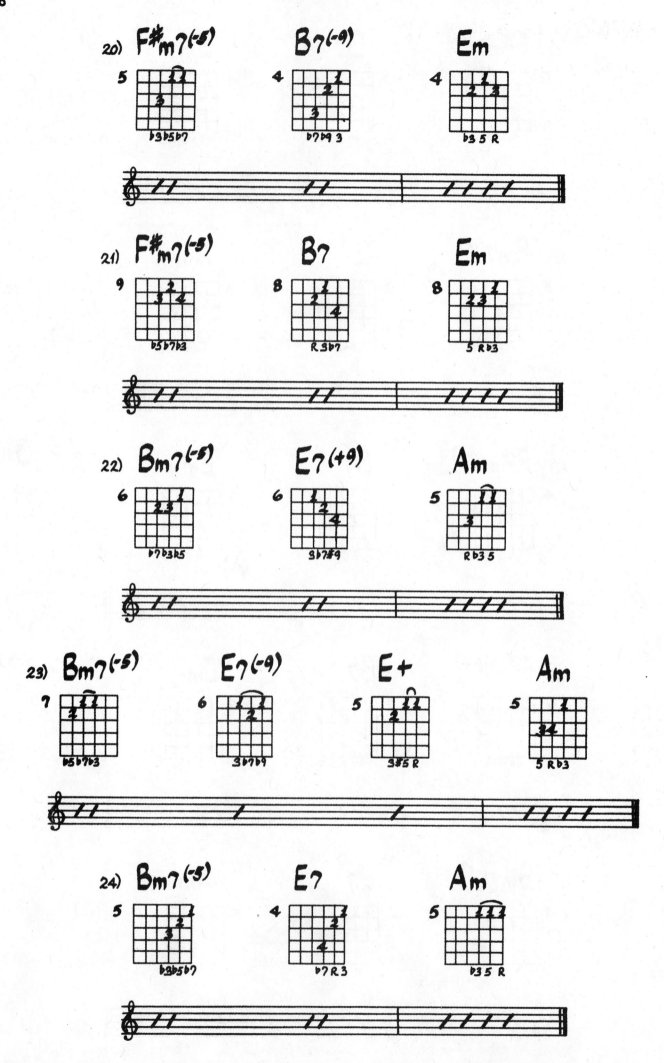

● MINOR (MAJOR 7)

- ● Keyboard Analysis:

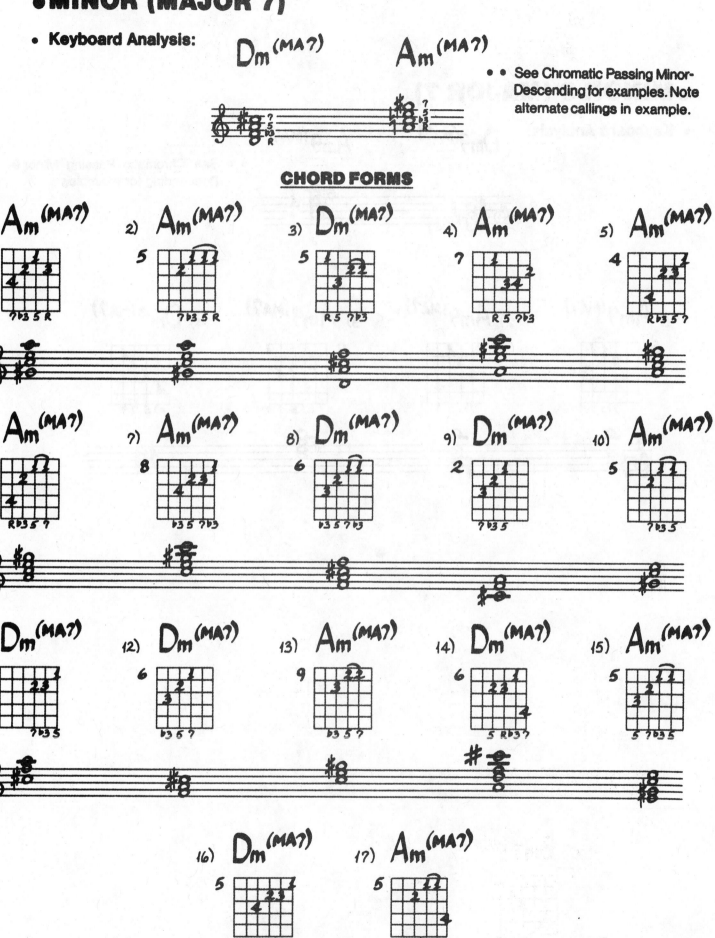

● ● See Chromatic Passing Minor-Descending for examples. Note alternate callings in example.

CHORD FORMS

●MINOR 9 (MAJOR 7)

● Keyboard Analysis:

●● See Chromatic Passing Minor 9-
Descending for examples.

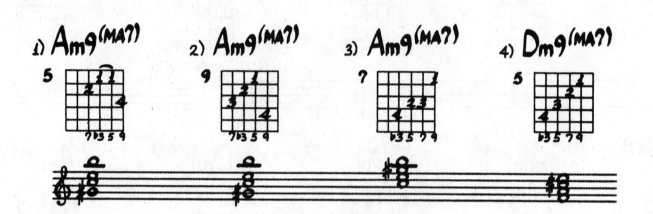

● PASSING MINOR CHORDS (Ascending)

Minor chords are typically passed from the ninth, root or fifth of the chord.
An ascending passing minor chord will be passed from the fiftn of the
chord up. A descending passing minor chord will be passed from the
ninth or root of the chord down. A chromatic, descending passing minor
will be passed from the root of the chord down. Refer to examples.

● ● Have a friend play the root note in the
bass in order to hear the complete
chord.

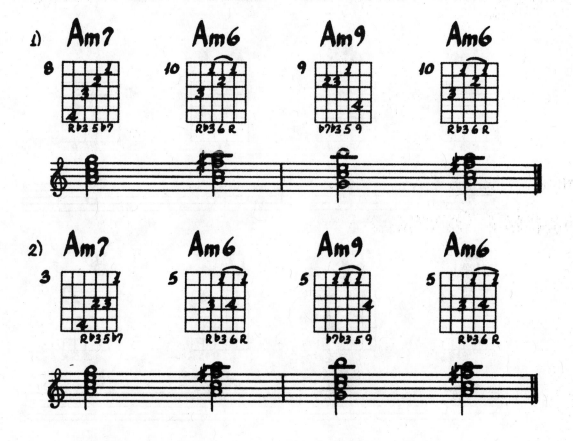

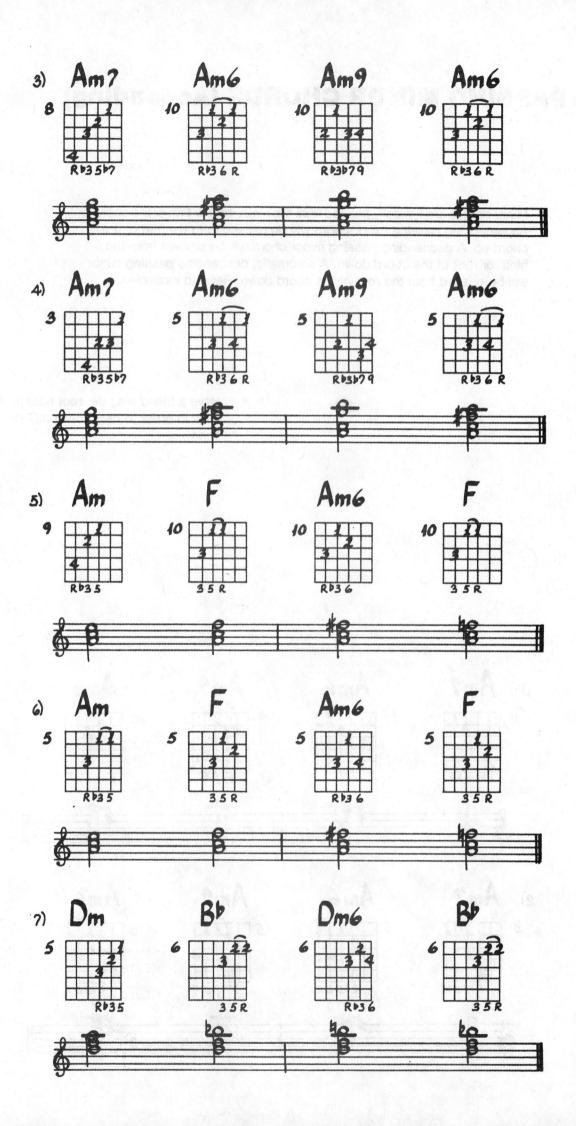

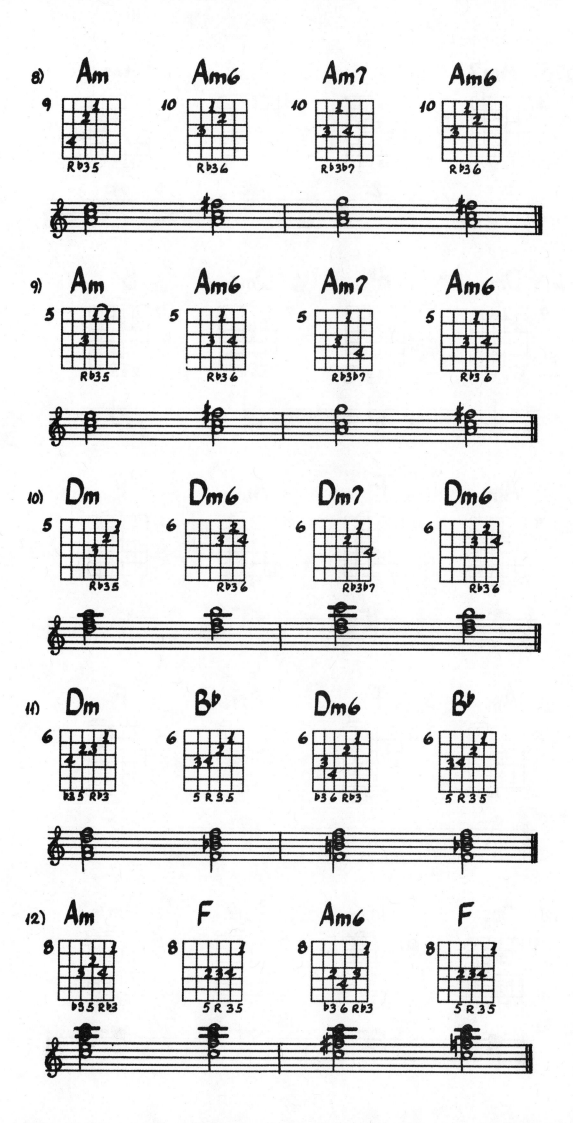

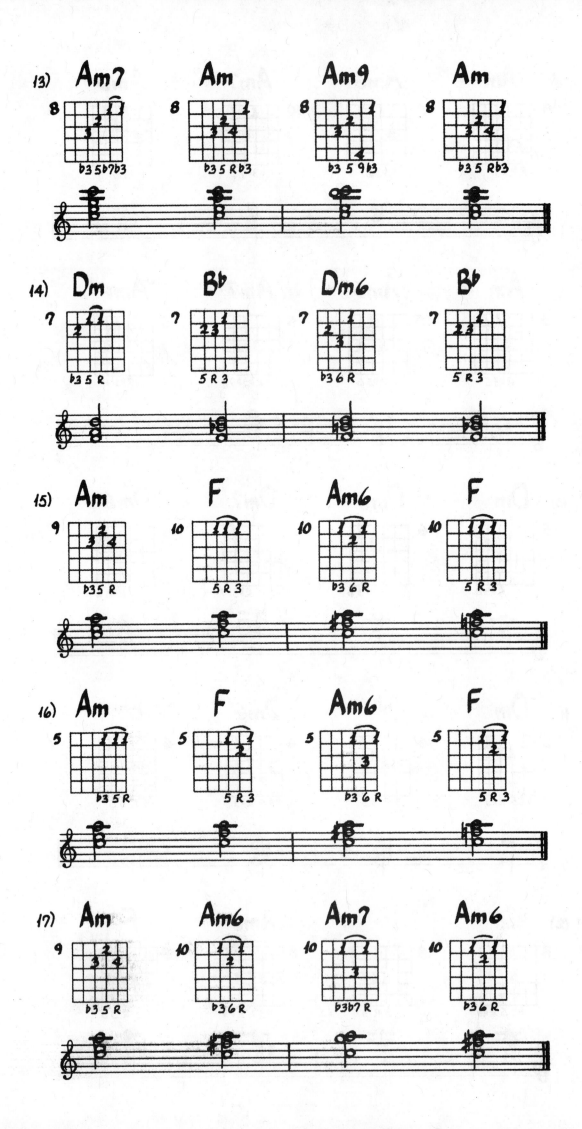

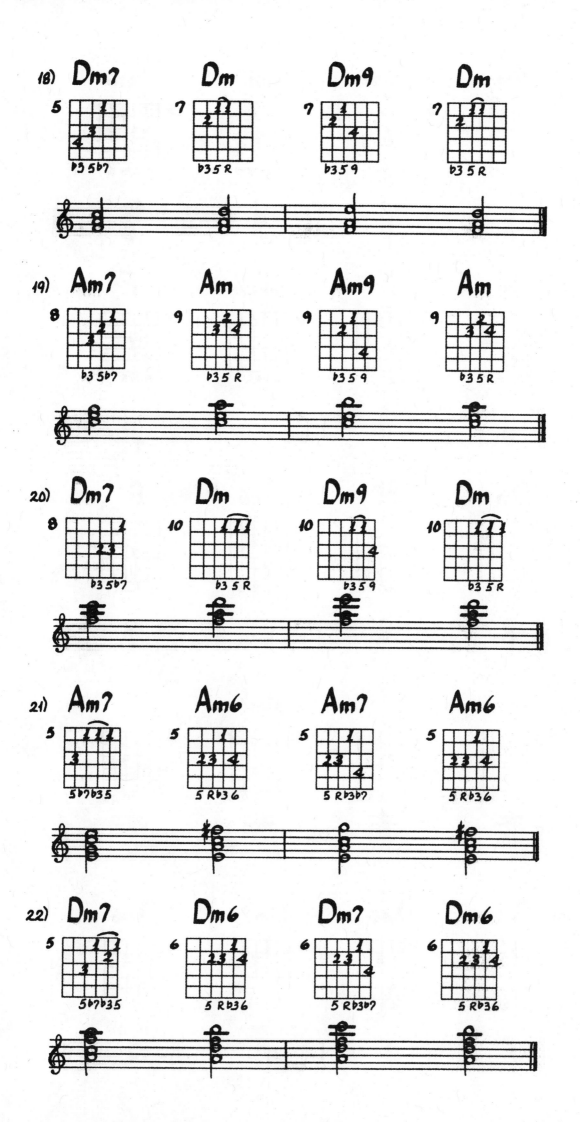

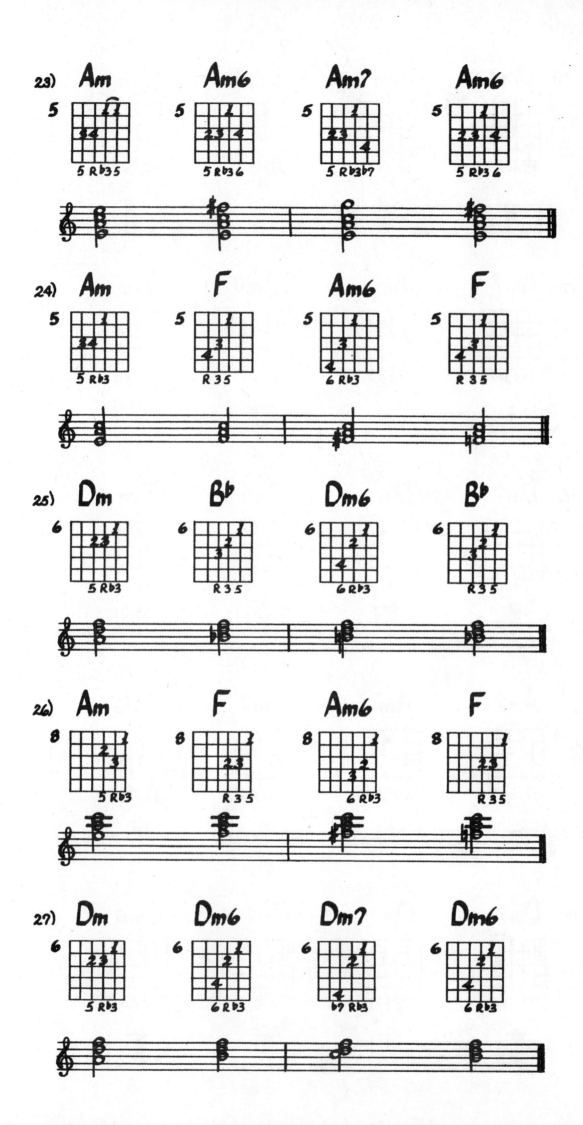

96

●CHROMATIC PASSING MINOR CHORDS
(Descending)

● ● Have a friend play the root note in the
bass in order to hear the complete
chord.

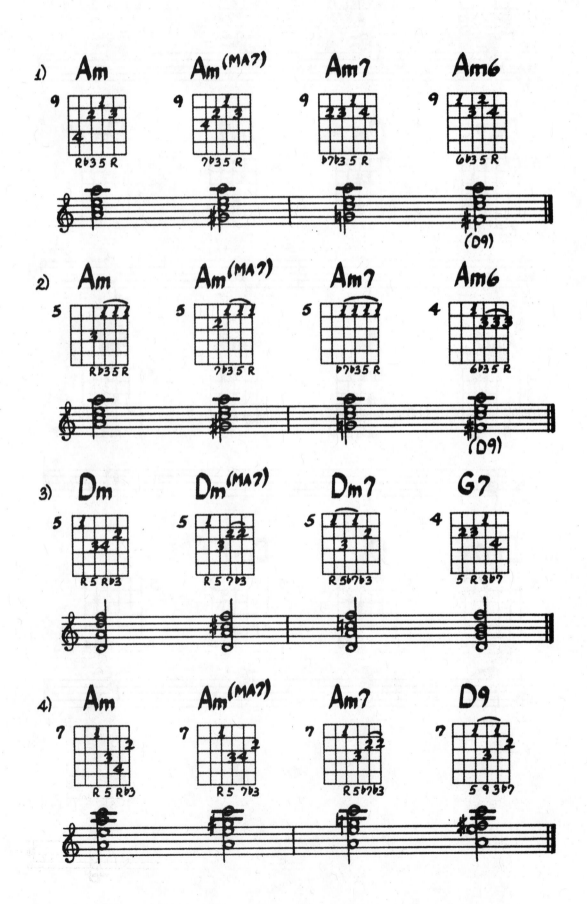

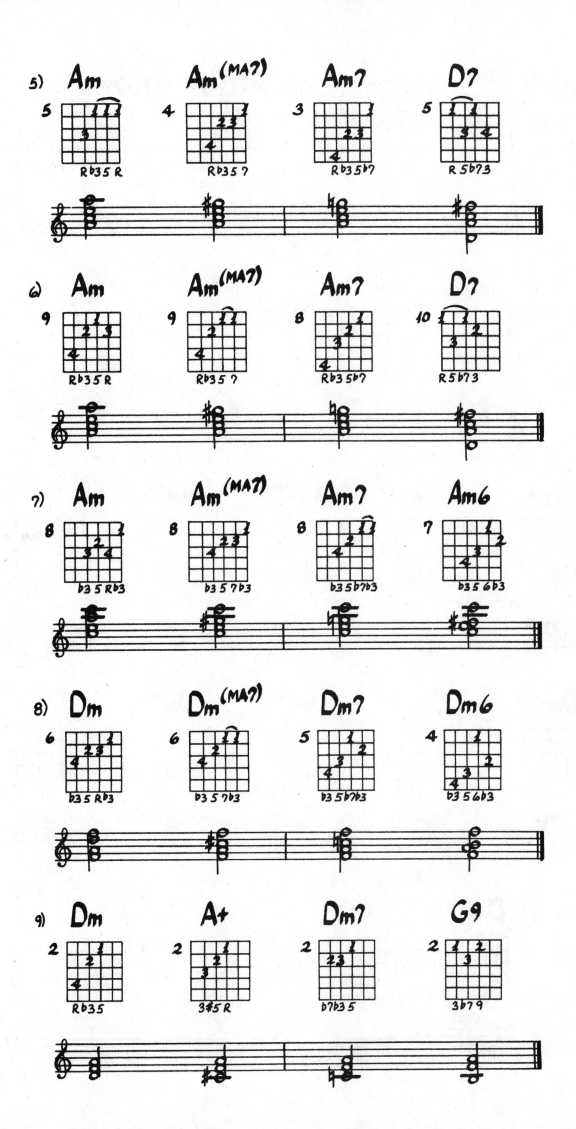

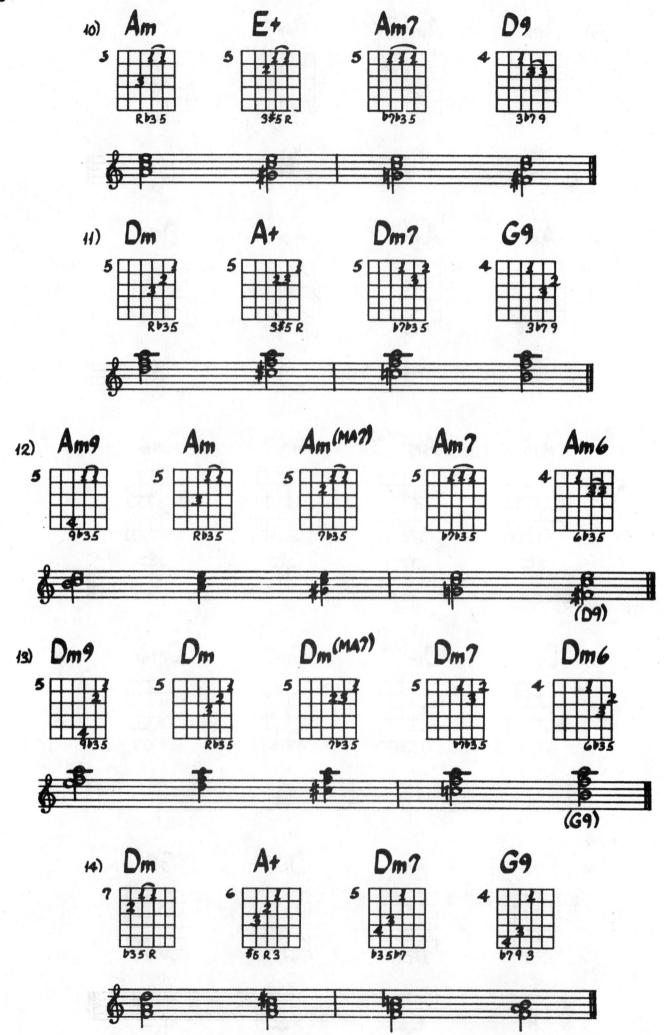

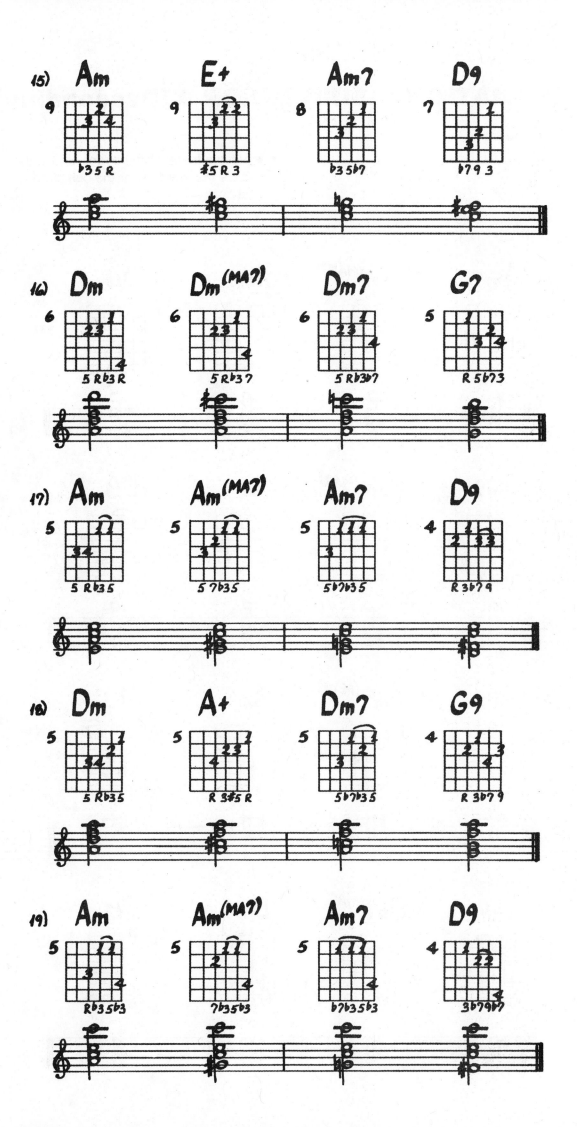

●CHROMATIC PASSING MINOR 9 (Descending)

• • • Have a friend play the root note in the bass in order to hear the complete chord.

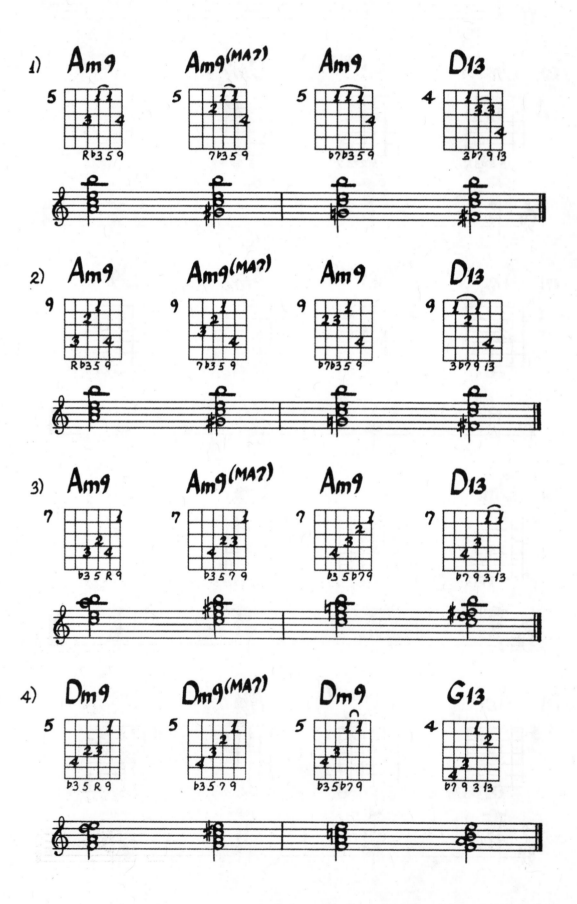

●DIATONIC PASSING MINOR (Descending)

●● Have a friend play the root note in the bass in order to hear the complete chord.

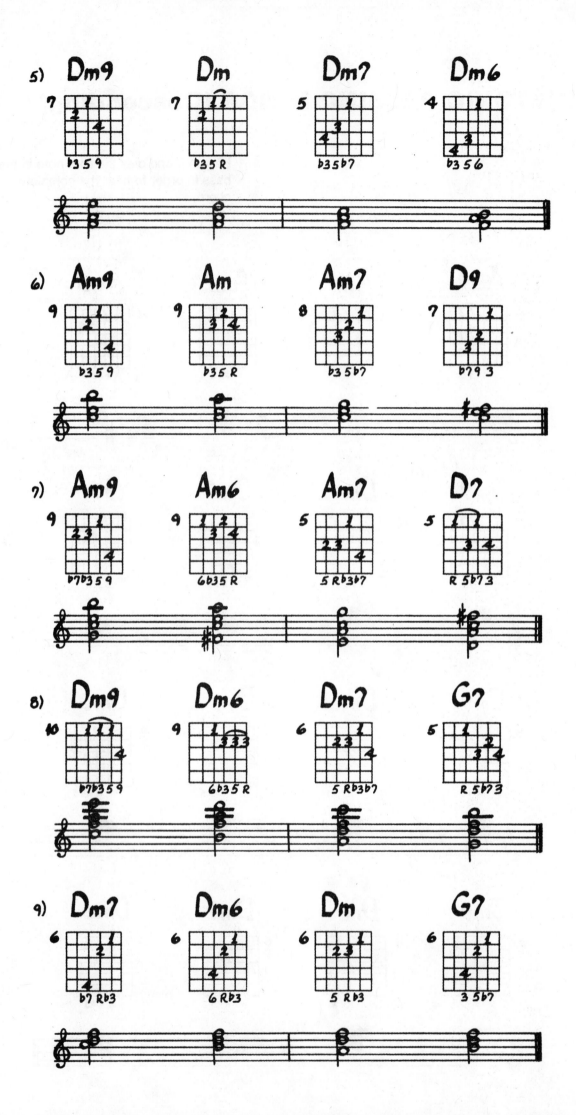

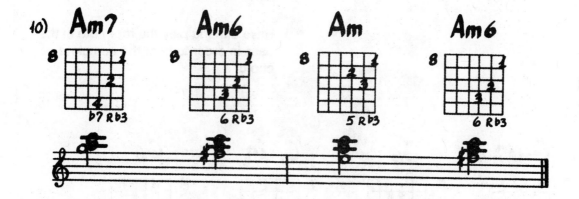

●PASSING MAJOR & MINOR COMBINED (Ascending)

• • Have a friend play the root note in the
bass in order to hear the complete
chord.

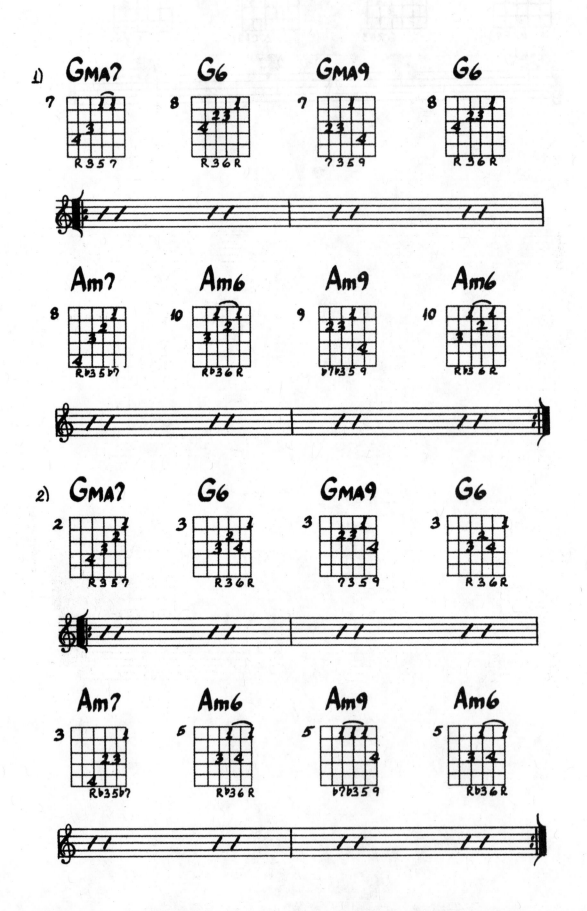

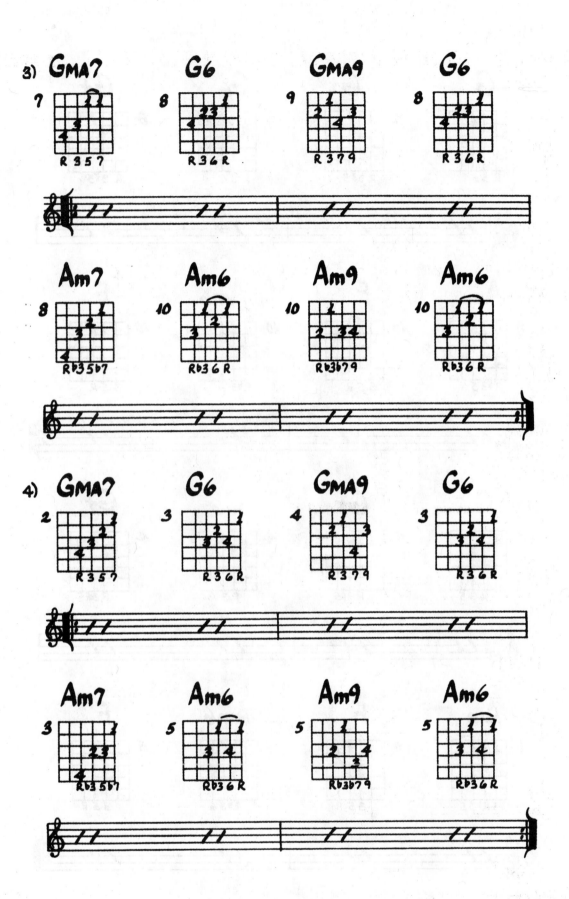

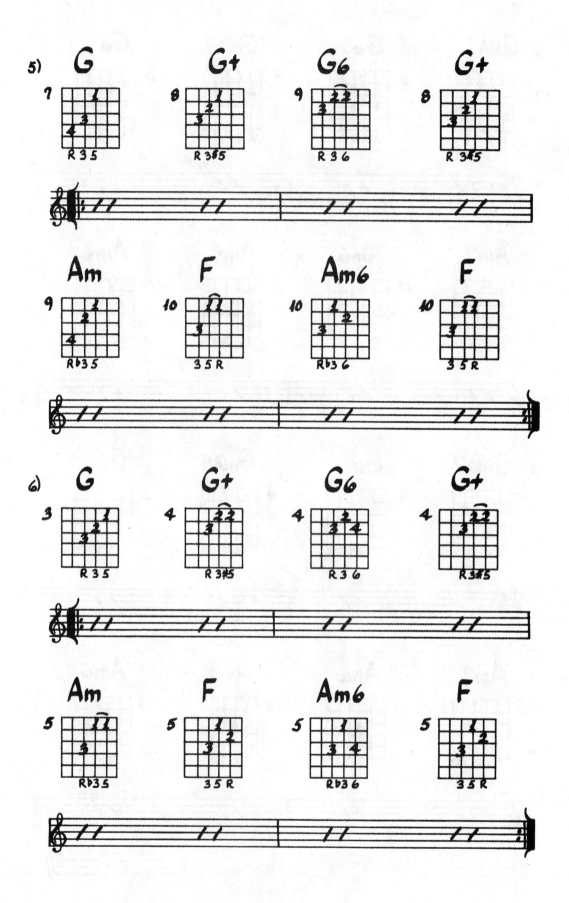

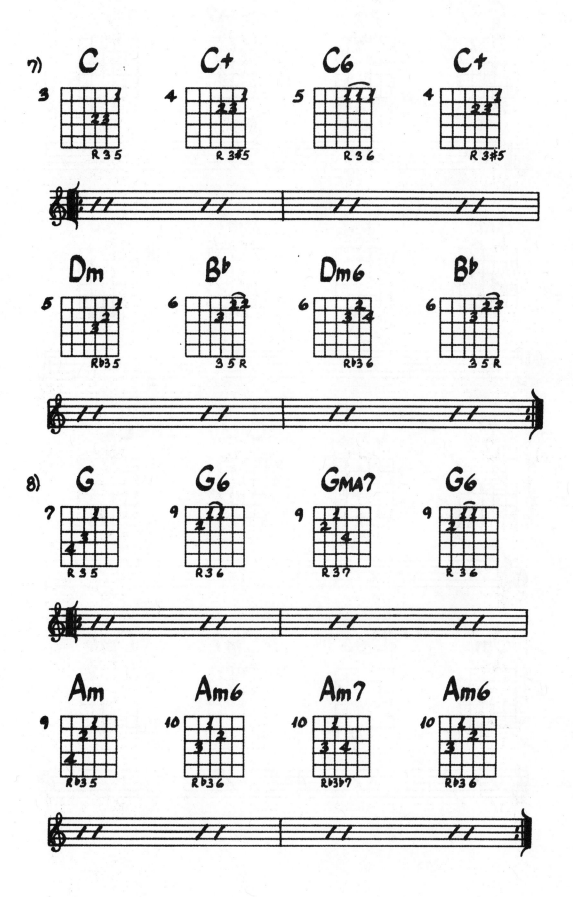

108

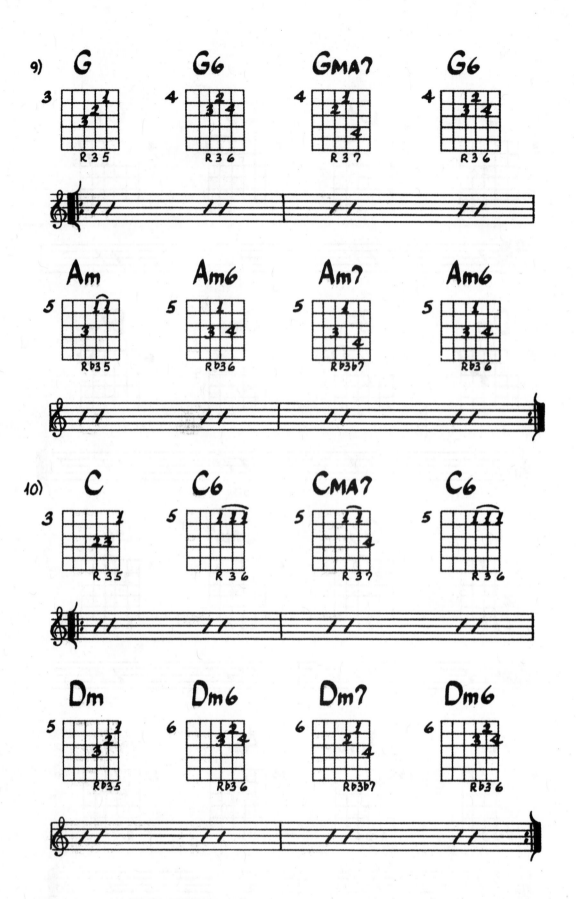

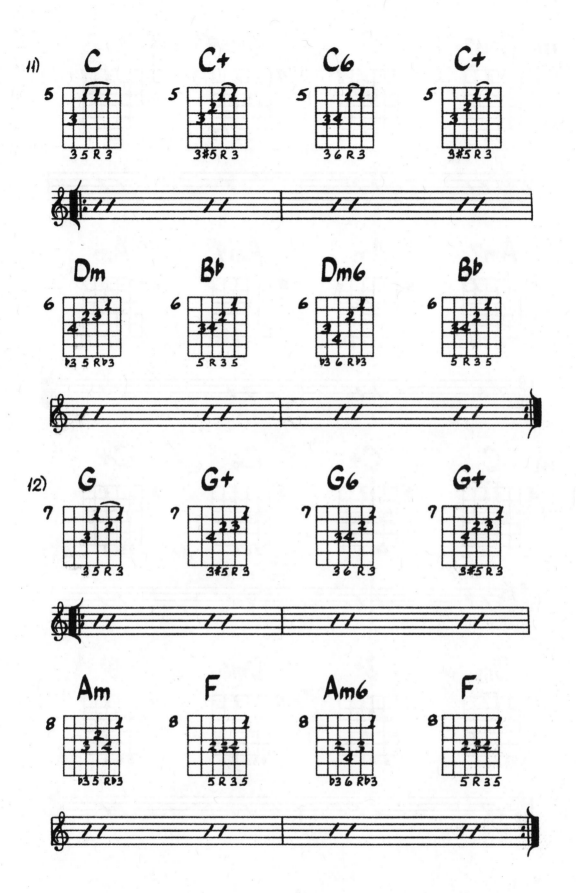

110

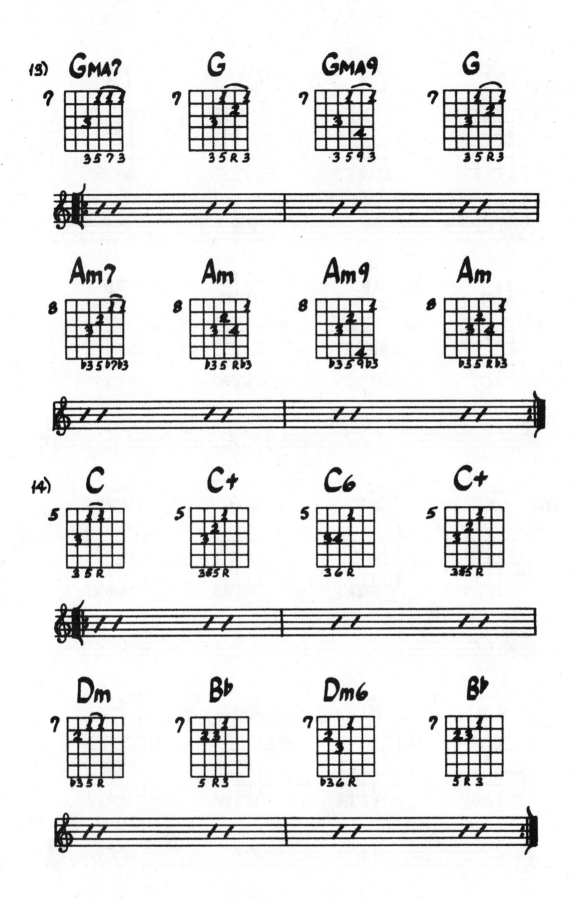

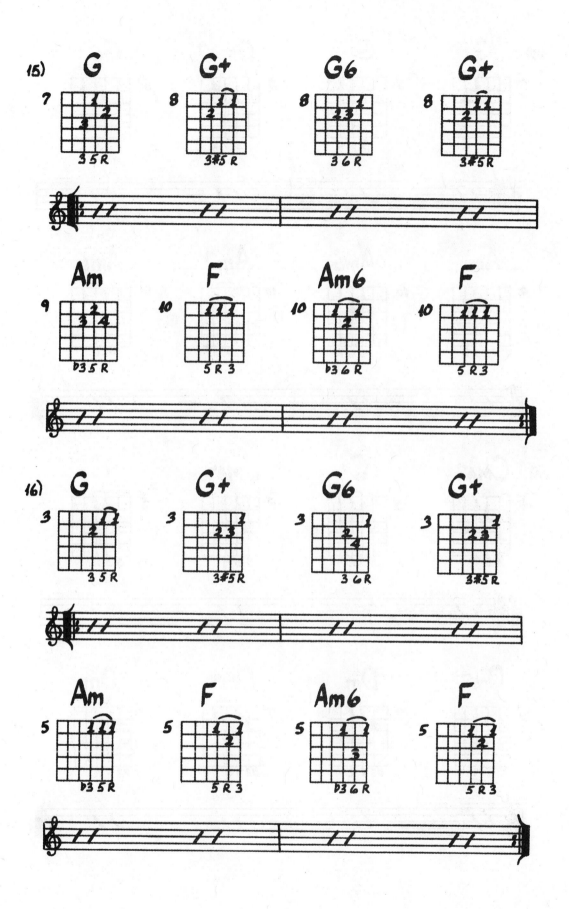

112

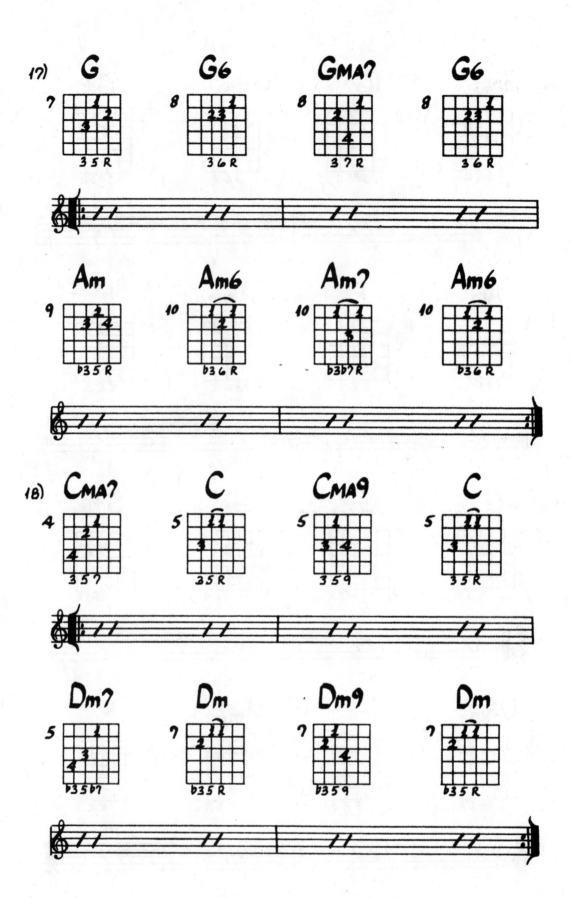

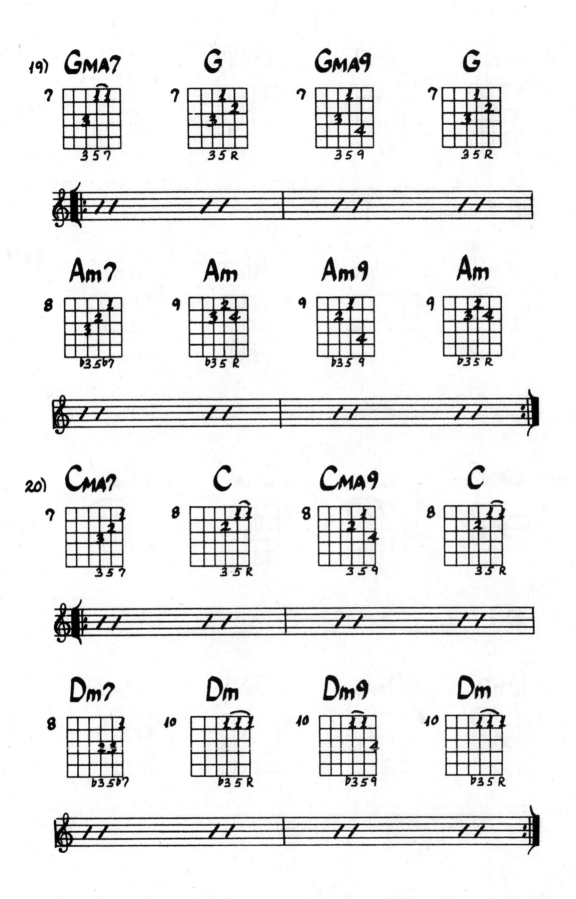

114

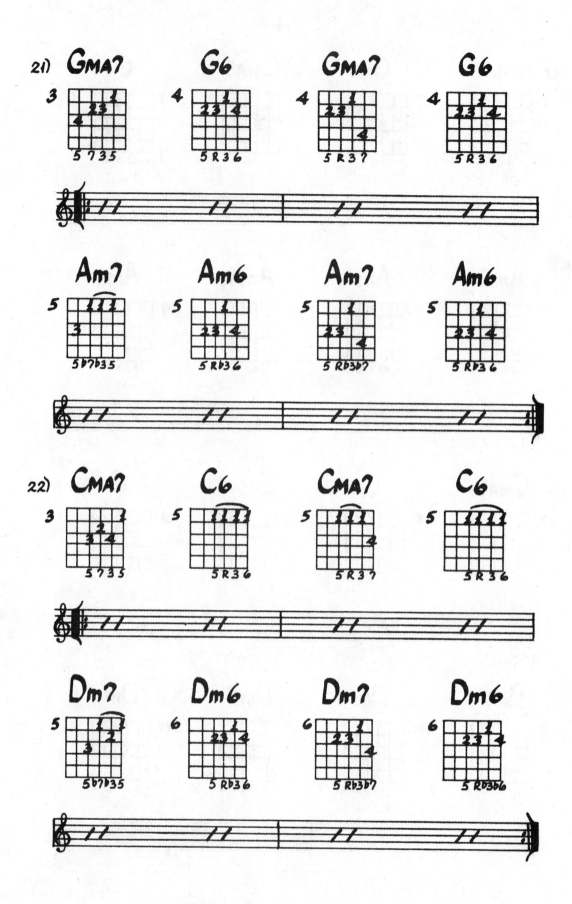

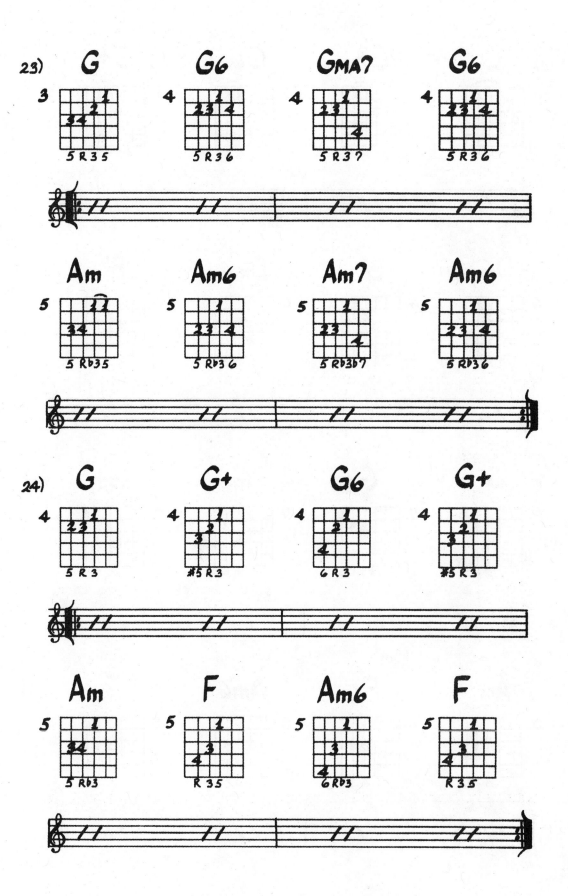

116

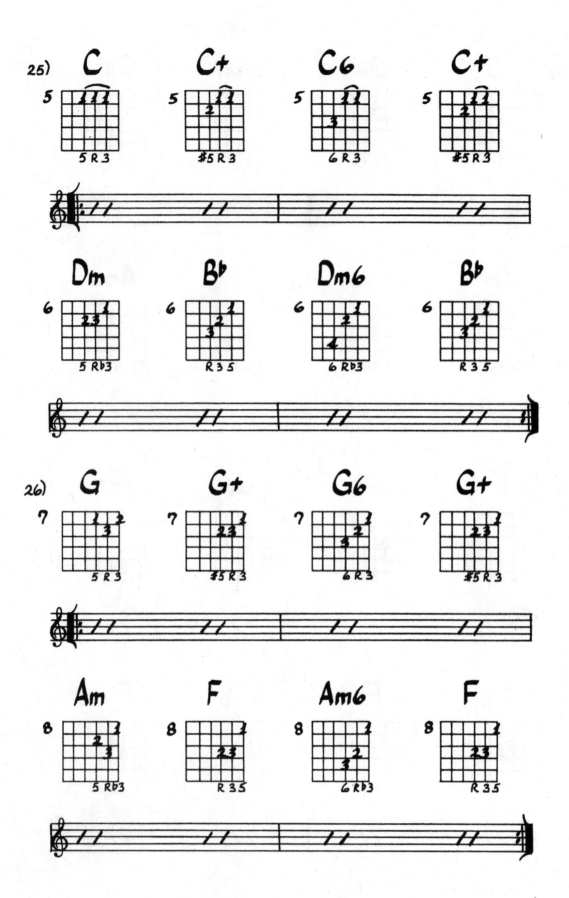

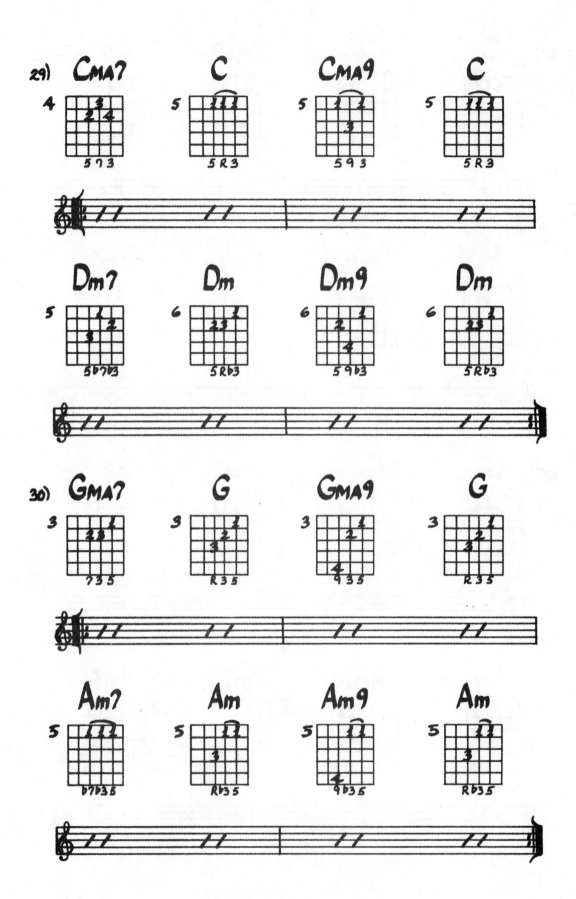

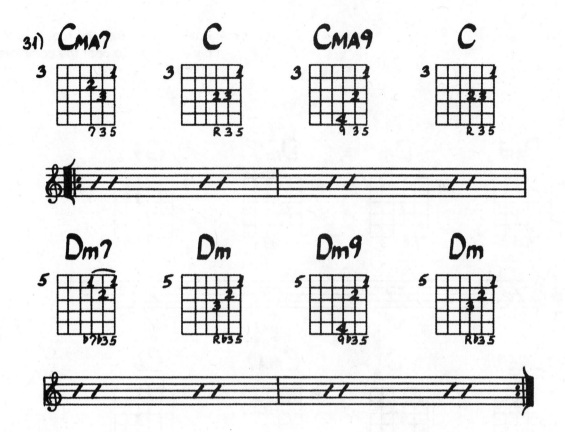

●PASSING MAJOR & MINOR COMBINED (Descending)

● ● Have a friend play the root note in the
bass in order to hear the complete
chord.

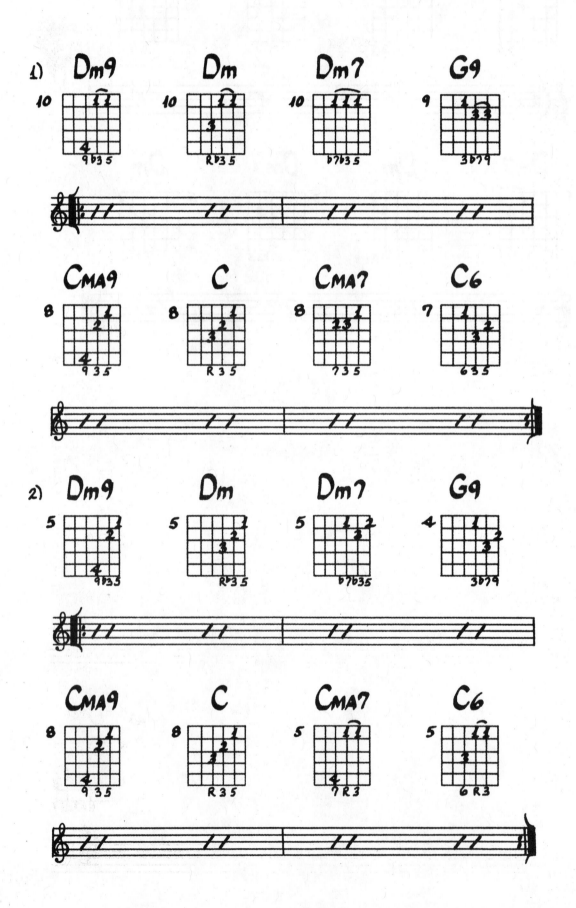

● DOMINANT 7

● Keyboard Analysis:

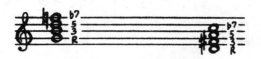

●● Have a friend play the root note in the bass in order to hear the complete chord.

CHORD FORMS

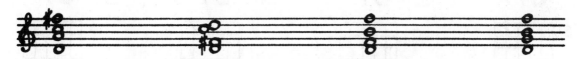

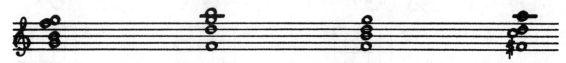

 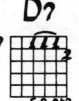
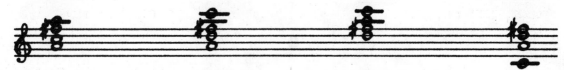

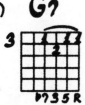 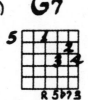 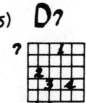

122

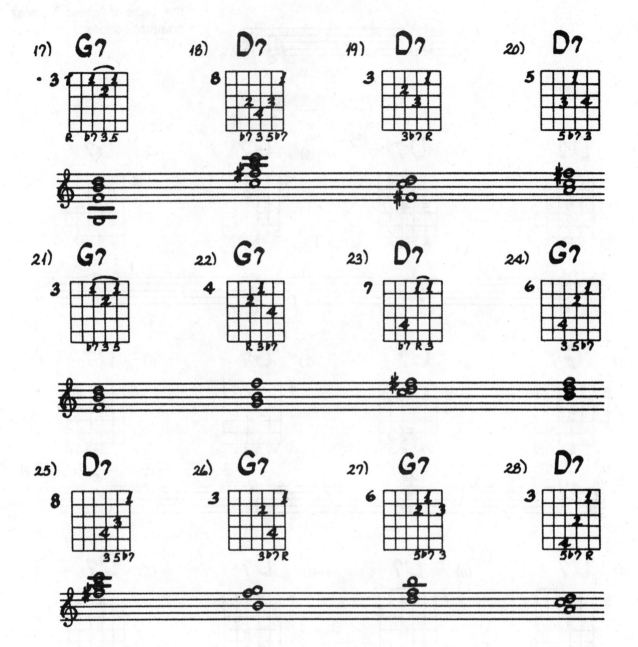

● DOMINANT 7 EXAMPLES

● ● Have a friend play the root note in the bass in order to hear the complete chord.

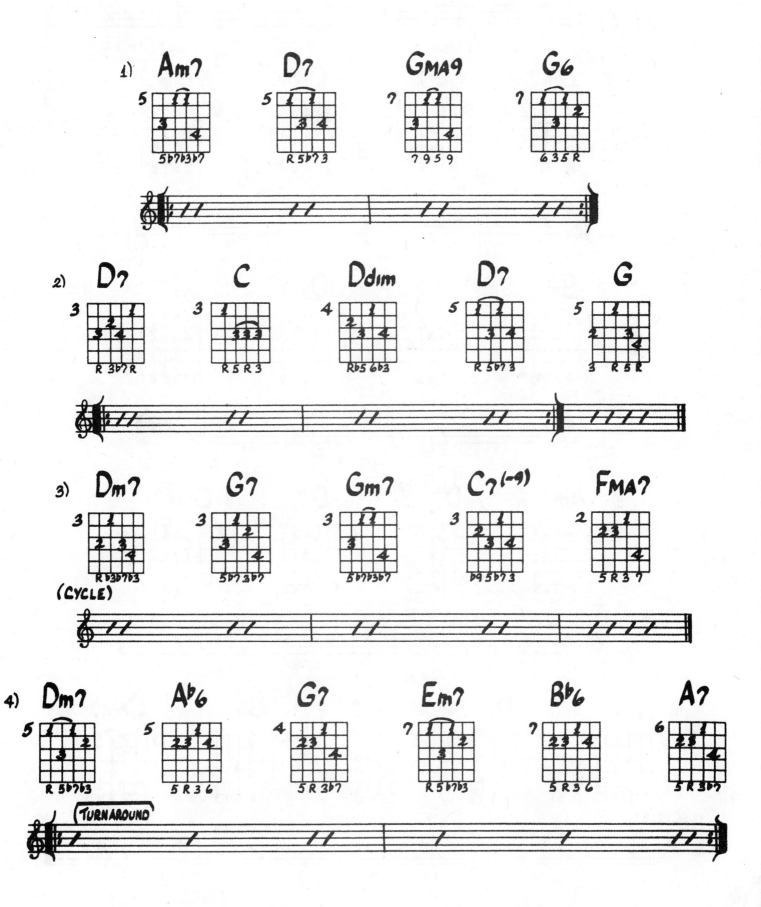

124

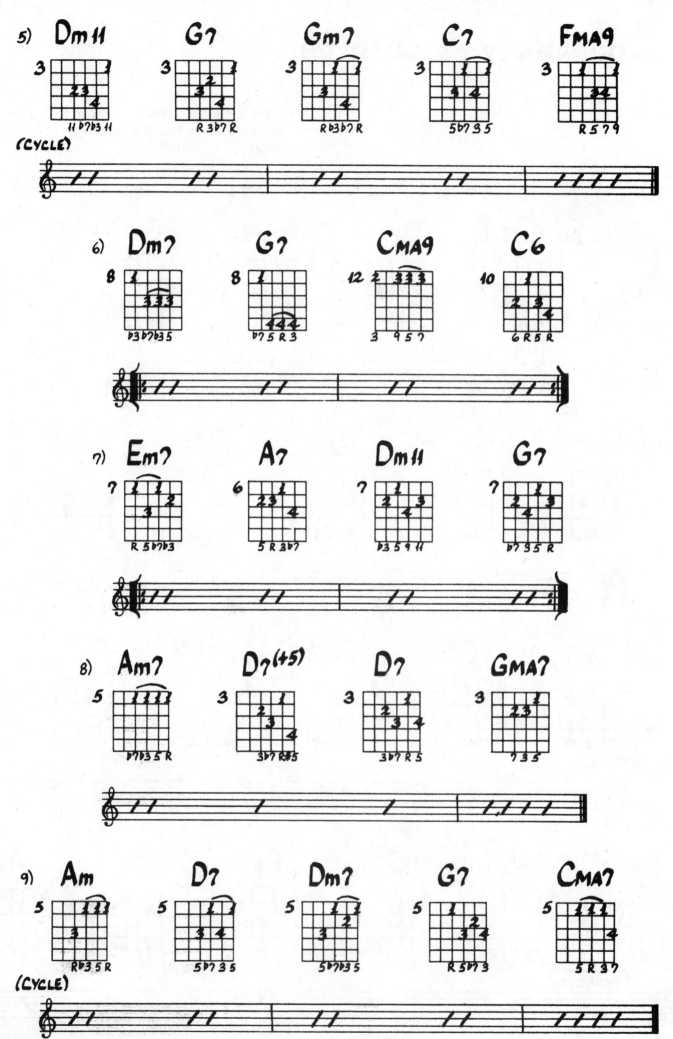

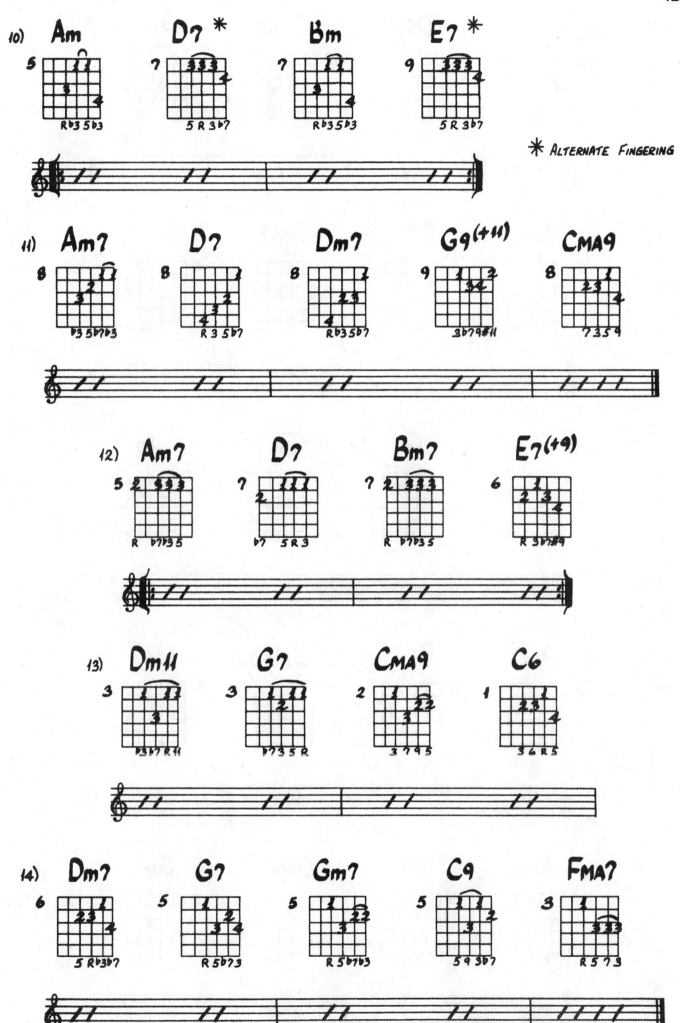

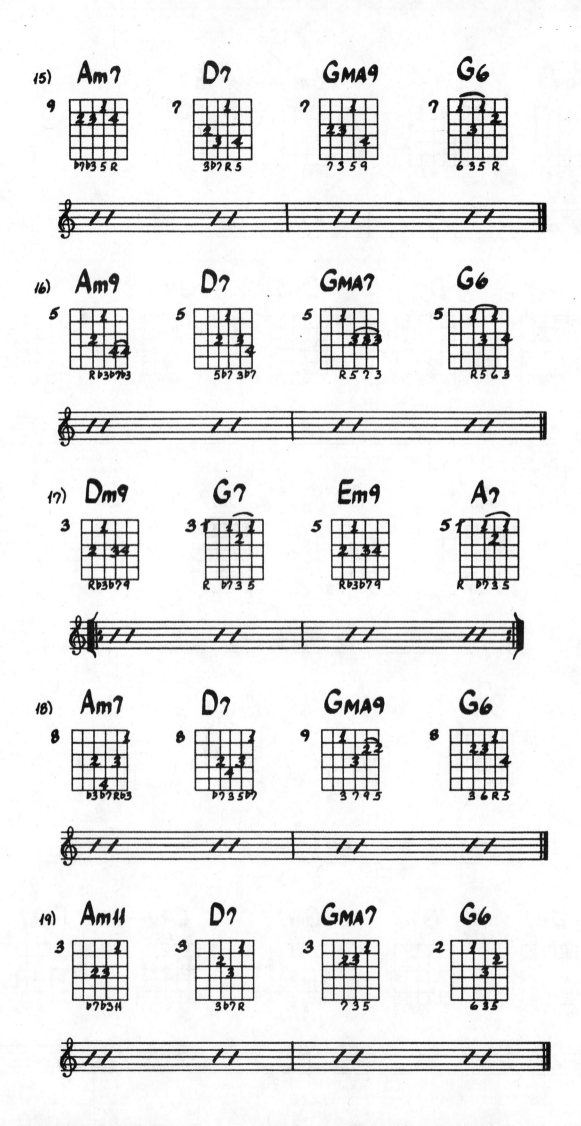

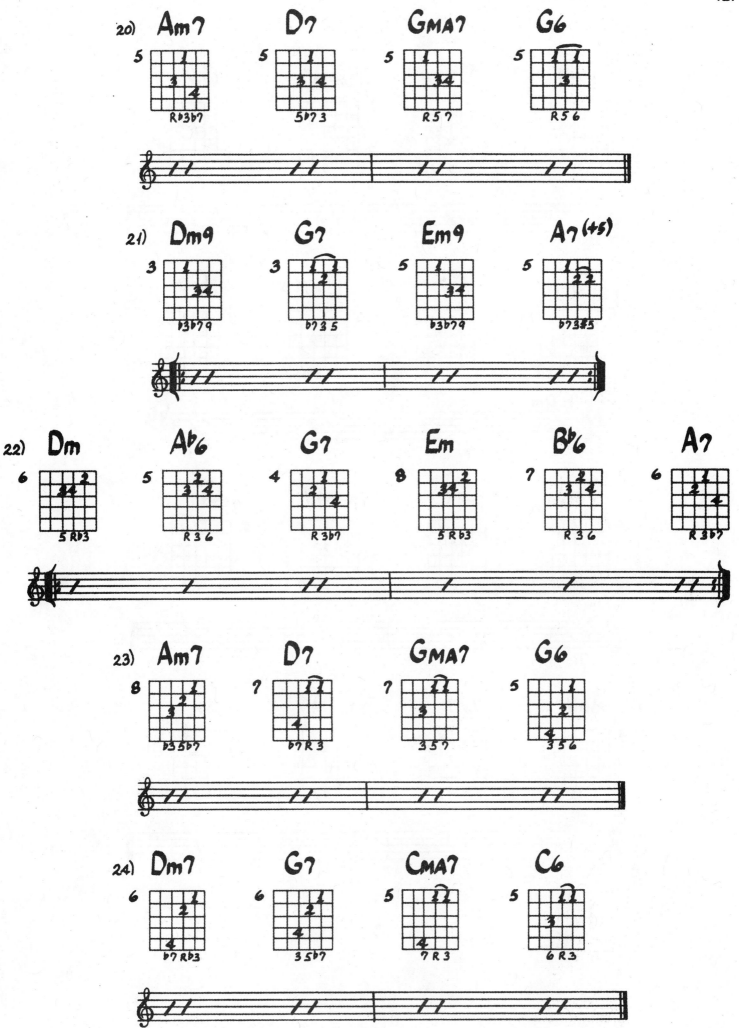

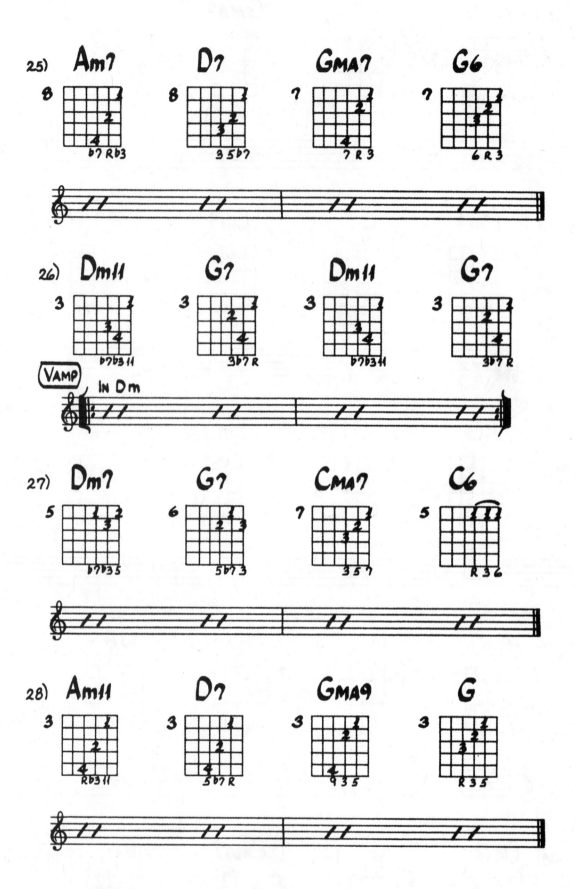

● DOMINANT 9

● Keyboard Analysis:

CHORD FORMS

130

● DOMINANT 9 EXAMPLES

•● Have a friend play the root note in the bass in order to hear the complete chord.

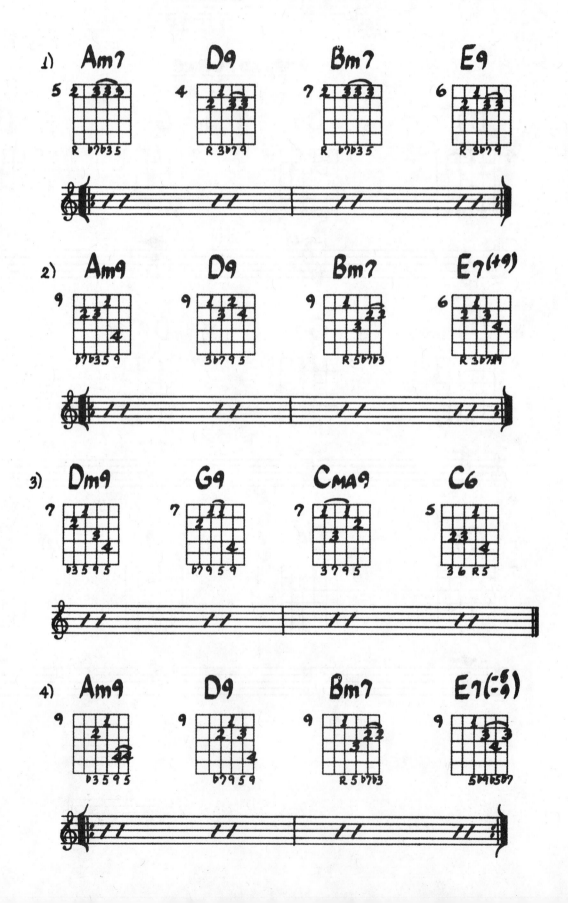

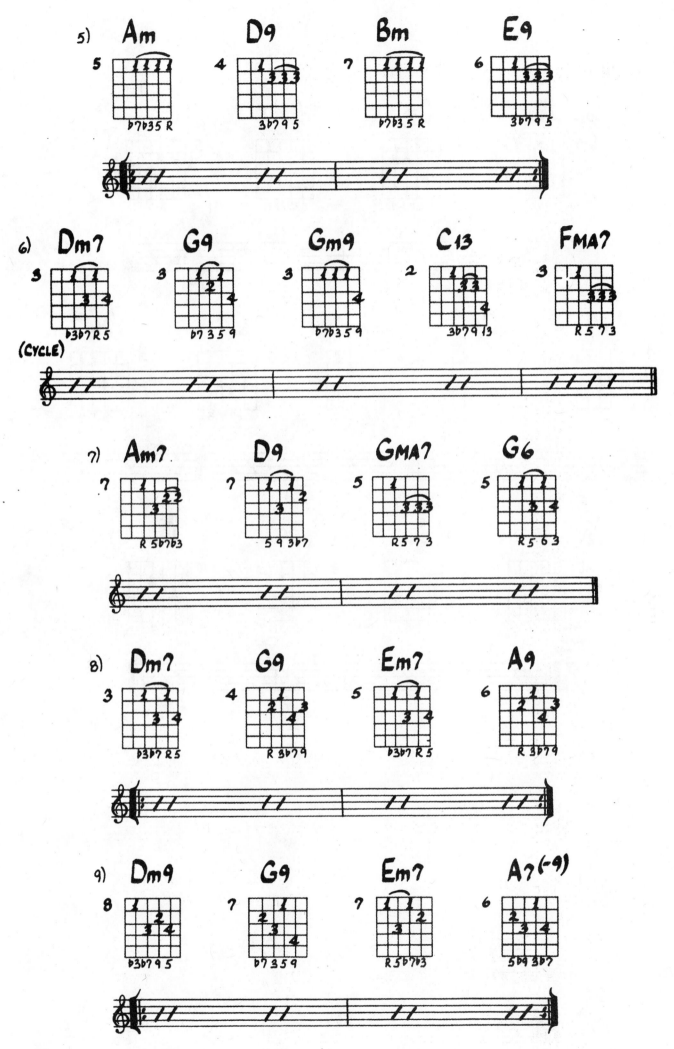

132

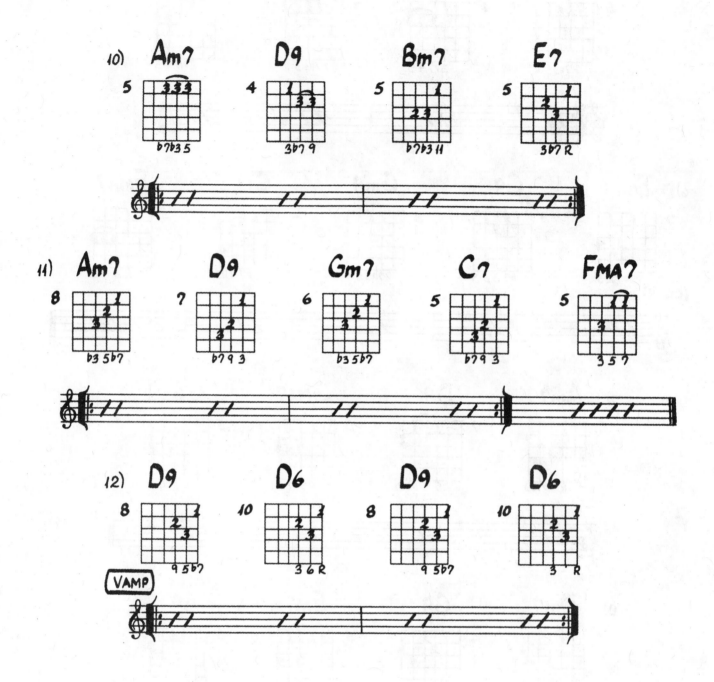

●DOMINANT 11

● Keyboard Analysis:

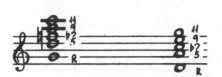

●● Also called Dom 7sus.
D11 can be called Am11.
G11 can be called Dm11.
Minor 11 chord forms 2, 14 and 20
are not Dom 11. See Minor 11 for
examples.

CHORD FORMS

1) **D11**

2) No Dom 11

3) **D11**

4) **G11**

5) **D11**

6) **G11**

7) **G11**

8) **D11**

9) **G11**

10) **D11**
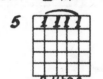

11) **G11**

12) **D11**

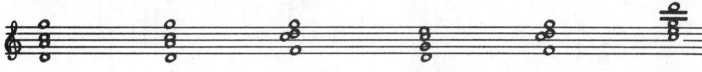

13) **G11**

14) No Dom 11

15) **D11**

16) **G11**

17) **G11**

18) **D11**

19) **D11**

20) No Dom 11

21) **G11**

22) **D11**

23) **G11**

24) **G11**

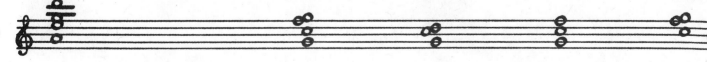

●DOMINANT 13

● **Keyboard Analysis:**

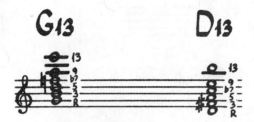

CHORD FORMS

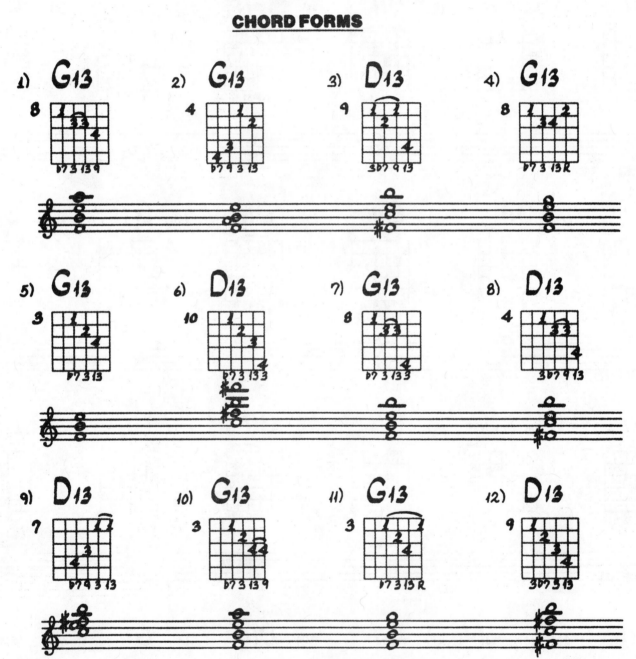

●DOMINANT 13 EXAMPLES

●● Have a friend play the root note in the bass in order to hear the complete chord.

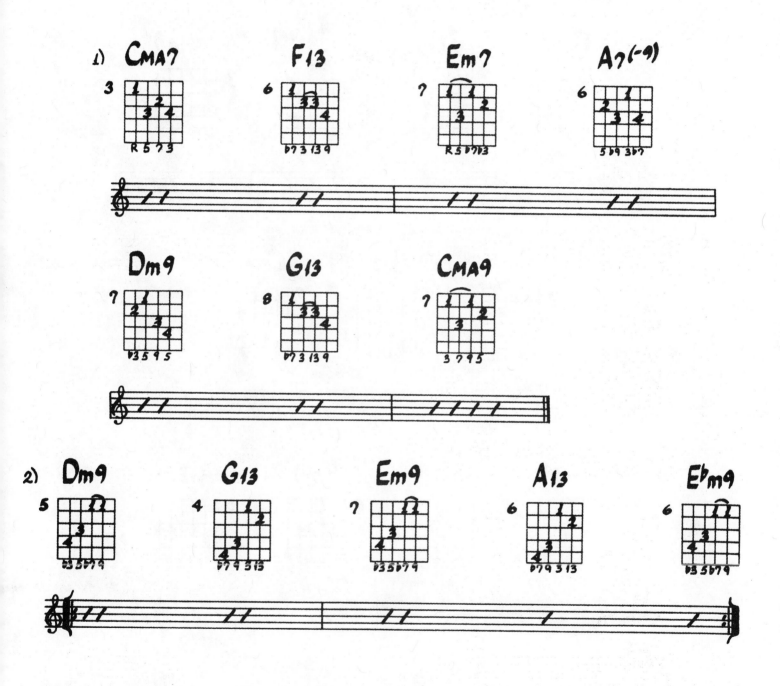

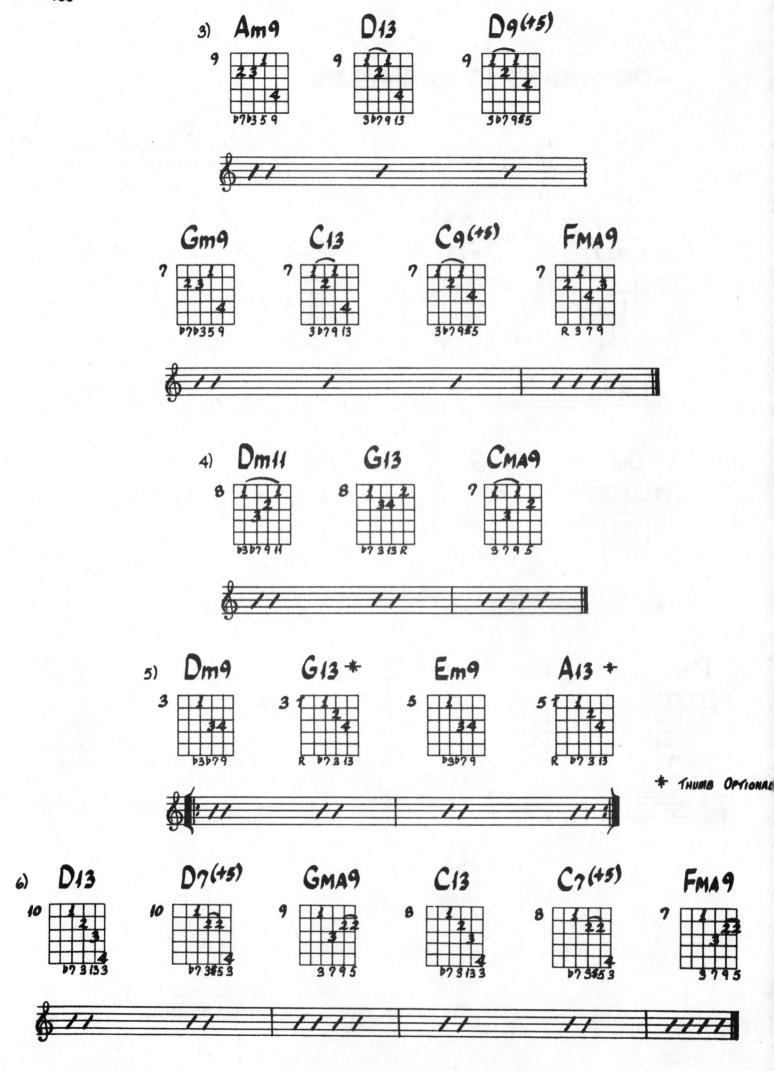

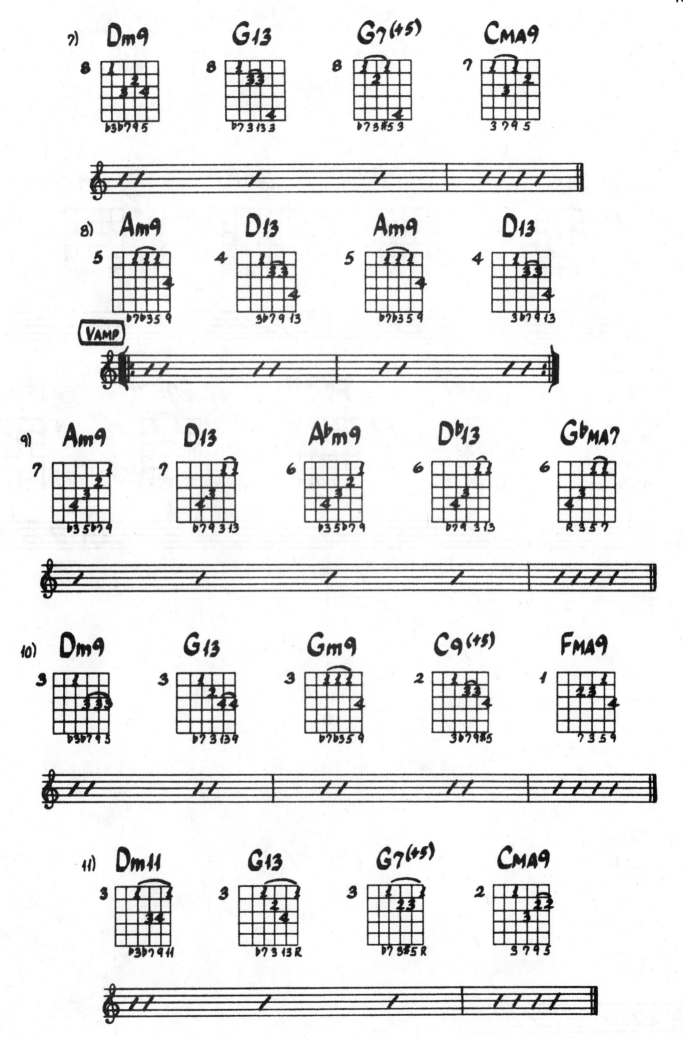

138

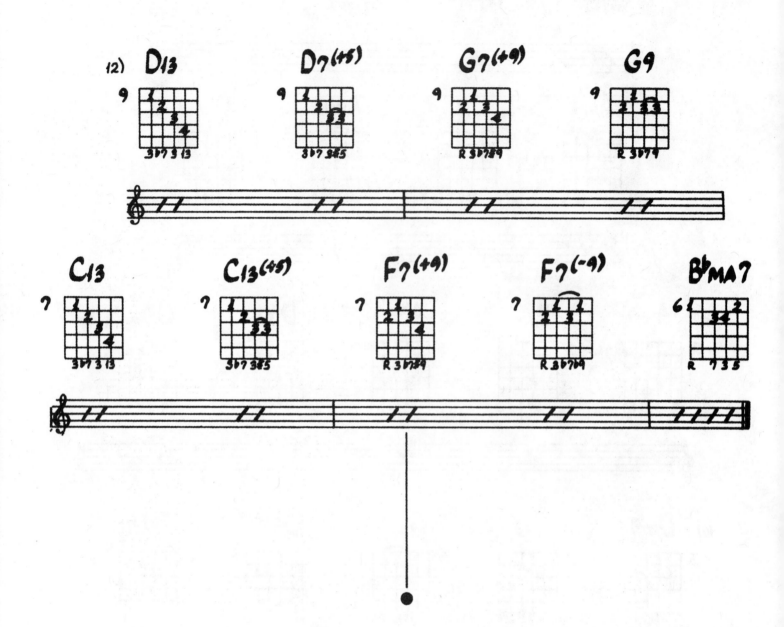

●DOMINANT 7♭5

● Keyboard Analysis:

CHORD FORMS

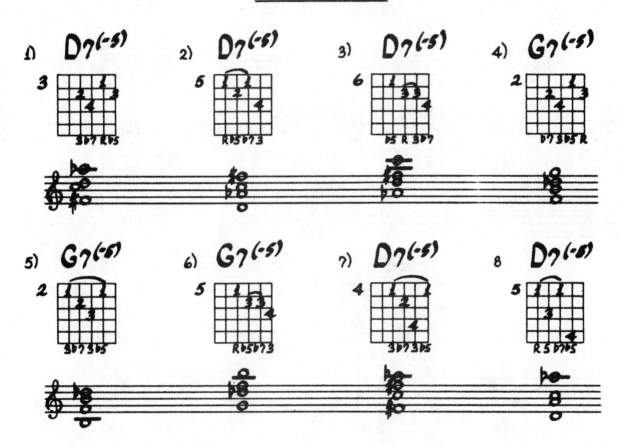

● DOMINANT 7♭5 EXAMPLES

● ● Have a friend play the root note in the bass in order to hear the complete chord.

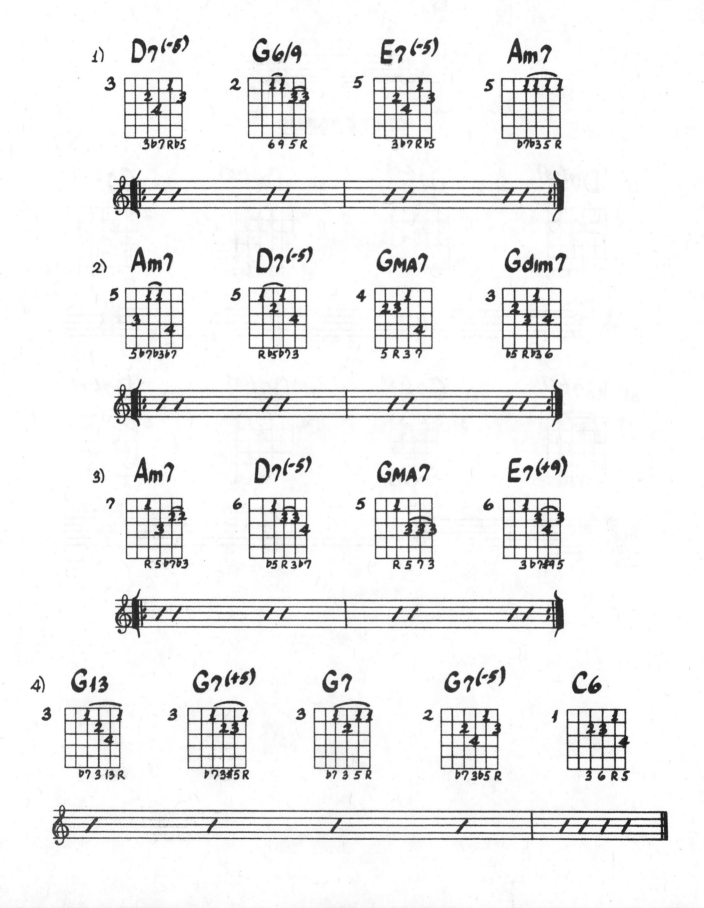

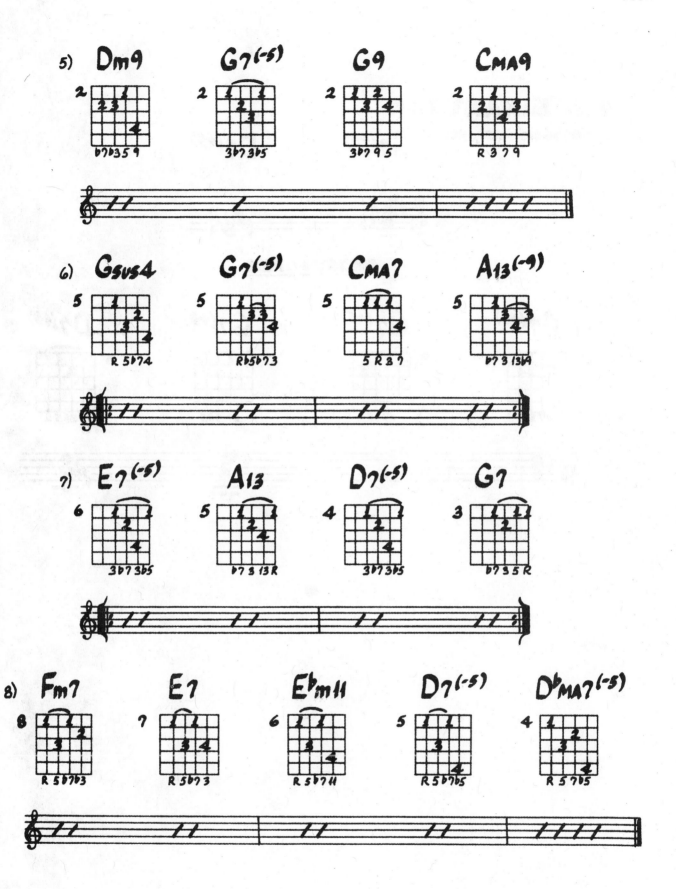

● DOMINANT 7+5
● **Keyboard Analysis:**

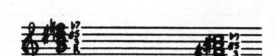

CHORD FORMS

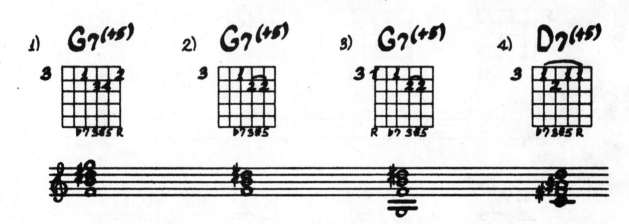

● DOMINANT 7+5 EXAMPLES

● ● Have a friend play the root note in the bass in order to hear the complete chord.

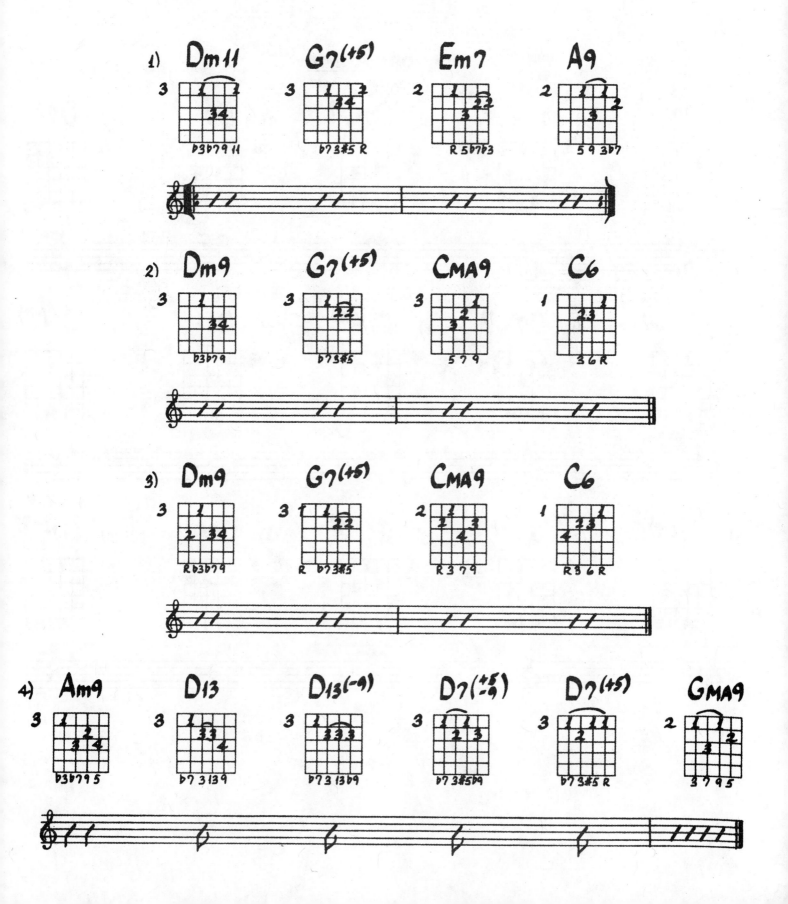

144

●DOMINANT 7♭9

● Keyboard Analysis:

CHORD FORMS

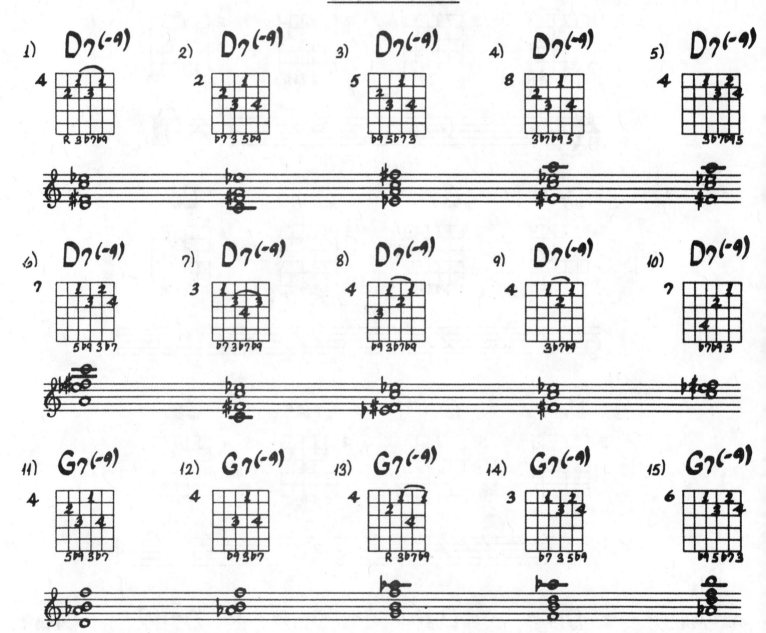

• DOMINANT 7♭9 EXAMPLES

• • Have a friend play the root note in the bass in order to hear the complete chord.

TAGS

1) Am7(-5) D7(-9) Bm7(-5) E7(-9)

2) Am9 D7(-9) Gma9 E7(-9)

3) Am7 D7(-9) Gma7 G6

4) Am7 D7(-9) Gma9 E7(-9)

146

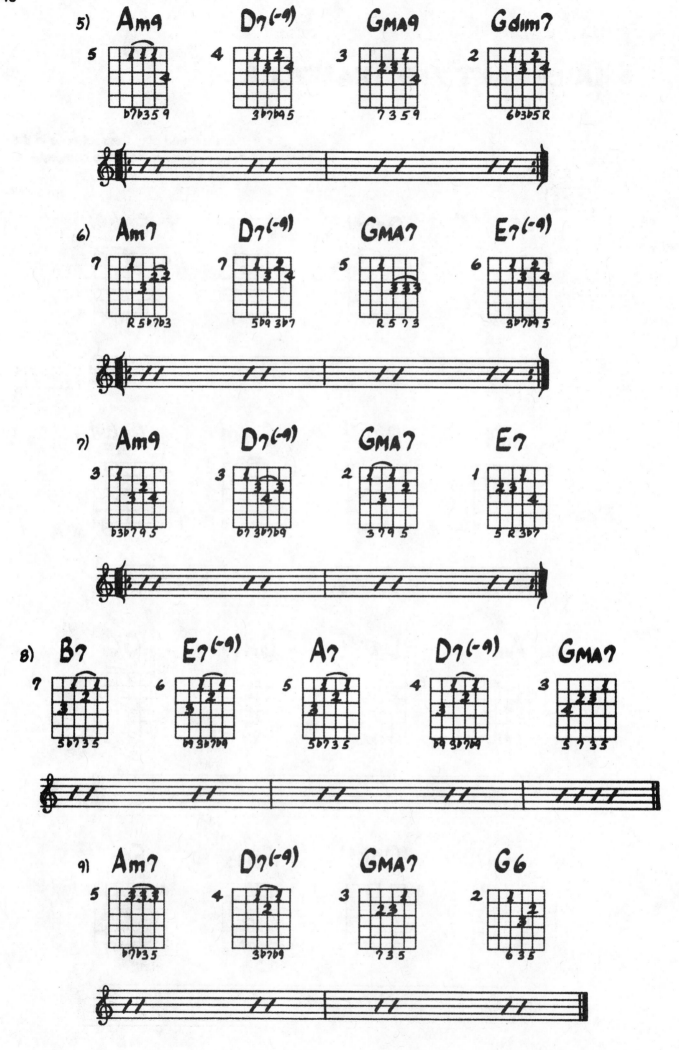

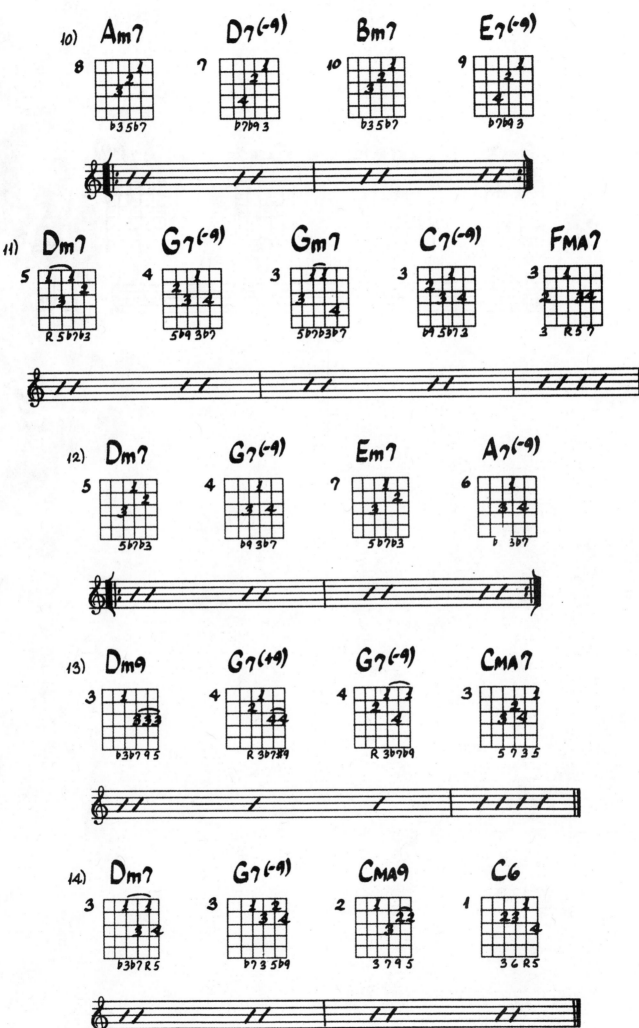

148

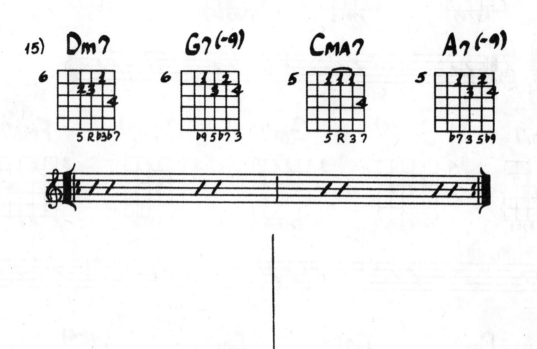

● MAJOR (♭9)

● **Keyboard Analysis:**

$G_{MA}^{(-9)}$ $D_{MA}^{(-9)}$

● ● This chord functions the same as a Dom 7♭9 chord.

CHORD FORMS

1) $D^{(-9)}$

2) $D^{(-9)}$

3) $D^{(-9)}$

4) $D^{(-9)}$

5) $D^{(-9)}$

6) $G^{(-9)}$

7) $G^{(-9)}$

8) $G^{(-9)}$

150

● MAJOR (♭9) EXAMPLES

● ● Have a friend play the root note in the bass in order to hear the complete chord.

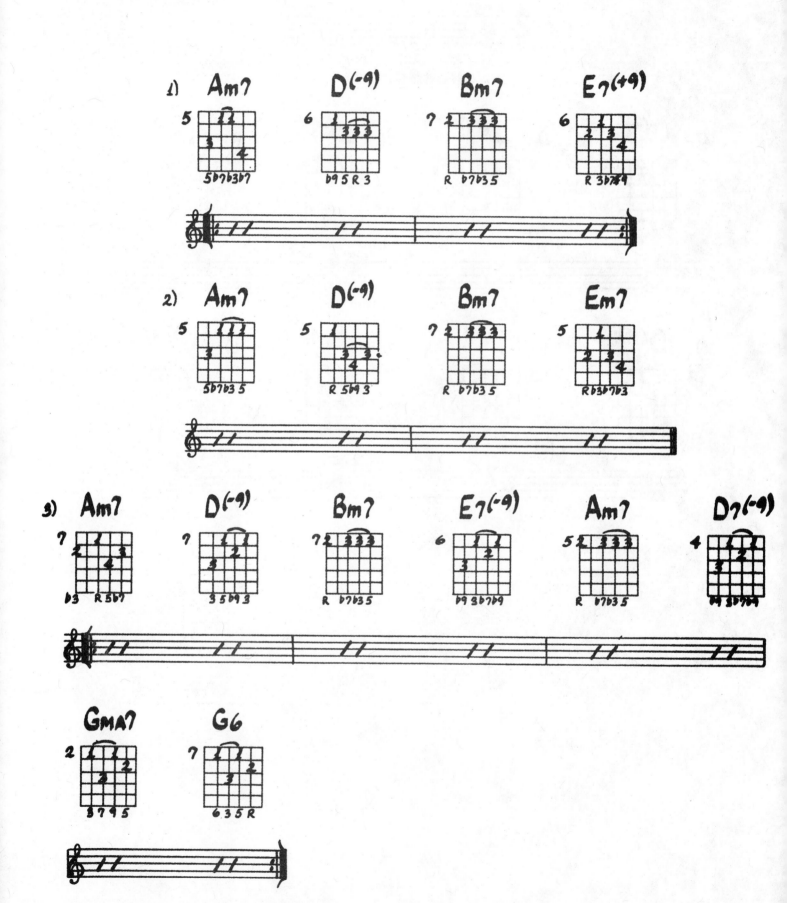

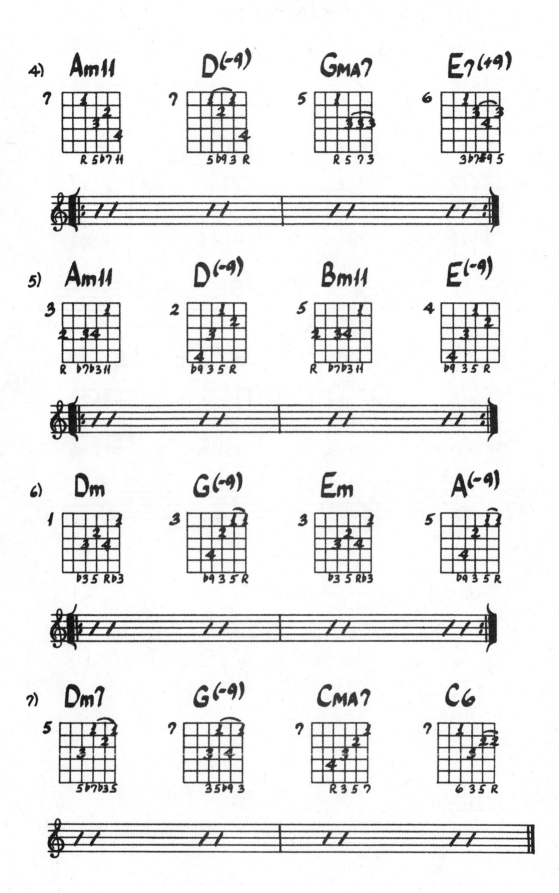

8)

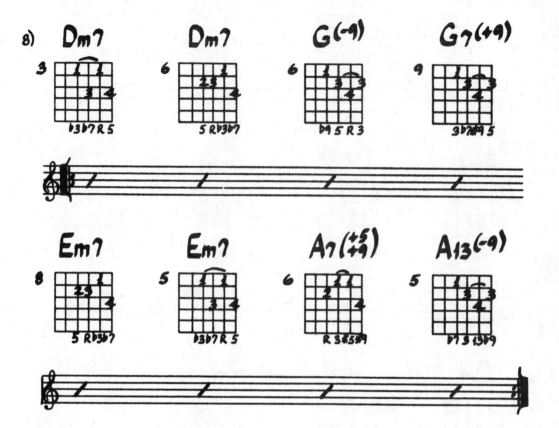

● DOMINANT 7+9

● Keyboard Analysis:

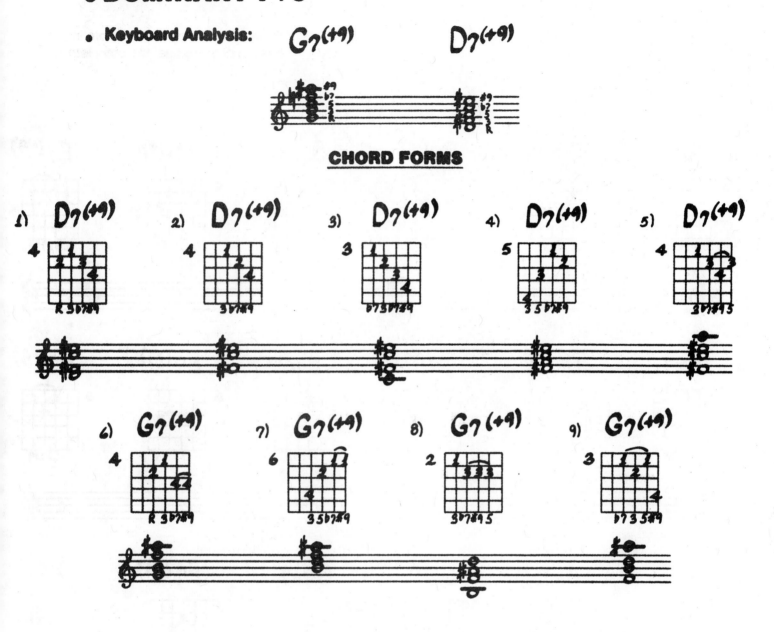

CHORD FORMS

• DOMINANT 7+9 EXAMPLES

• • Have a friend play the root note in the bass in order to hear the complete chord.

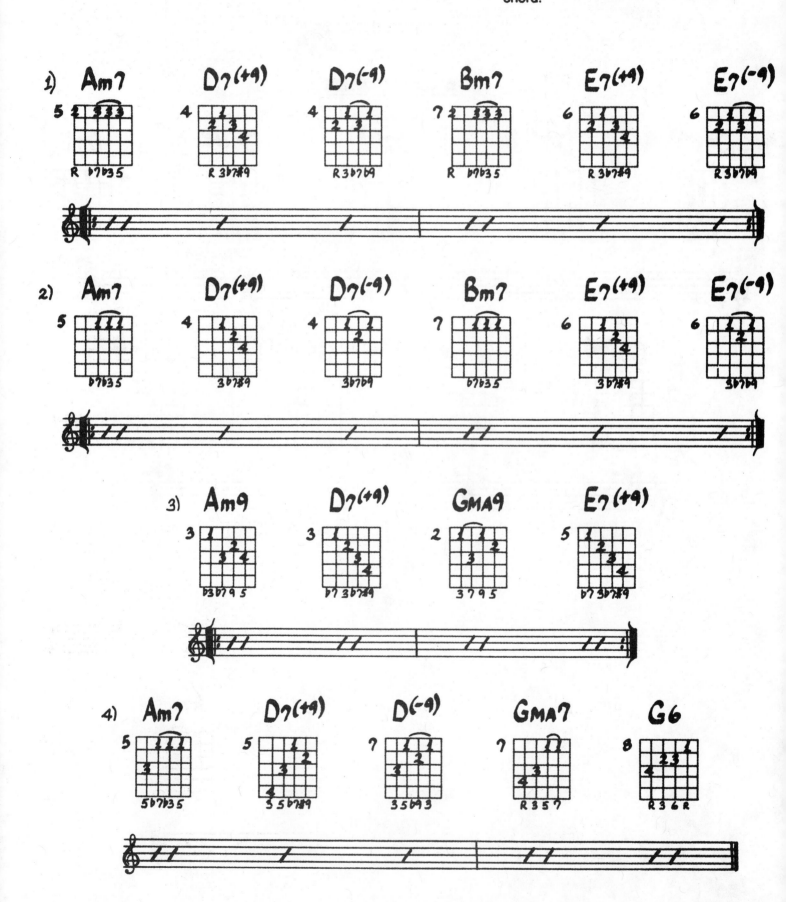

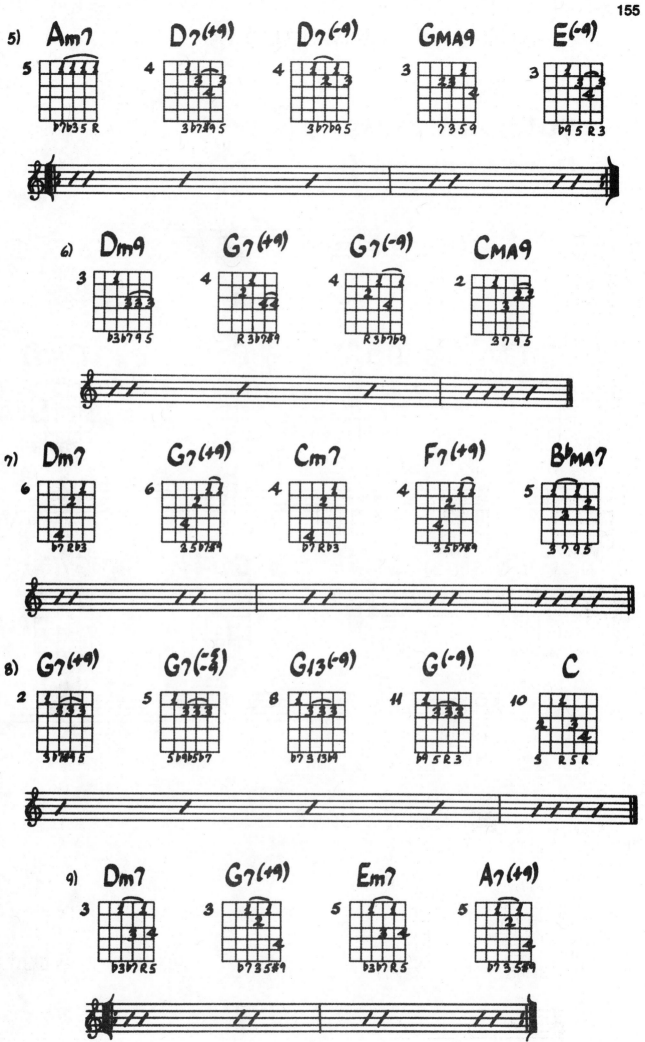

● DOMINANT 7♭5♭9

● Keyboard Analysis: G7(-⁵/₉) D7(-⁵/₉)

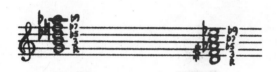

CHORD FORMS

1) G7(-⁵/₉) 2) D7(-⁵/₉) 3) G7(-⁵/₉) 4) G7(-⁵/₉)

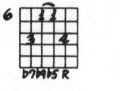

5) G7(-⁵/₉) 6) D7(-⁵/₉) 7) G7(-⁵/₉) 8) G7(-⁵/₉)

●

● DOMINANT 7♭5♭9 EXAMPLES

● ● Have a friend play the root note in the bass in order to hear the complete chord.

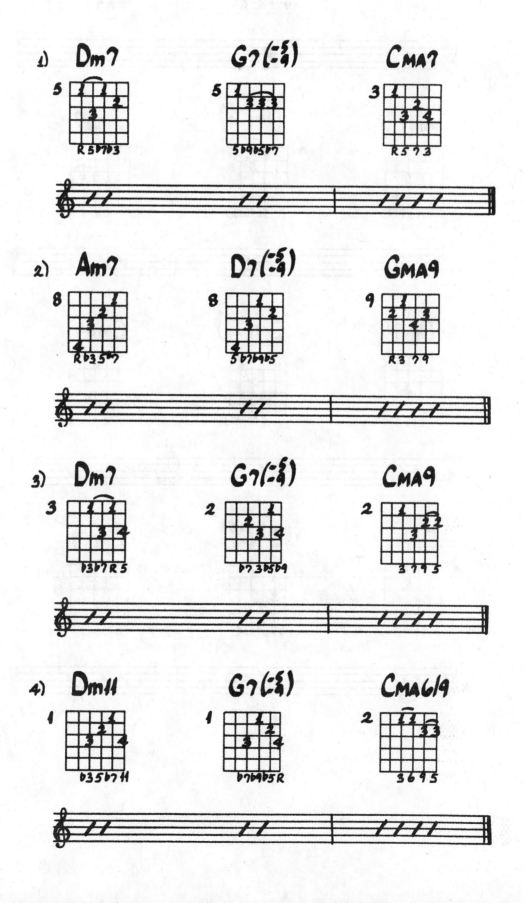

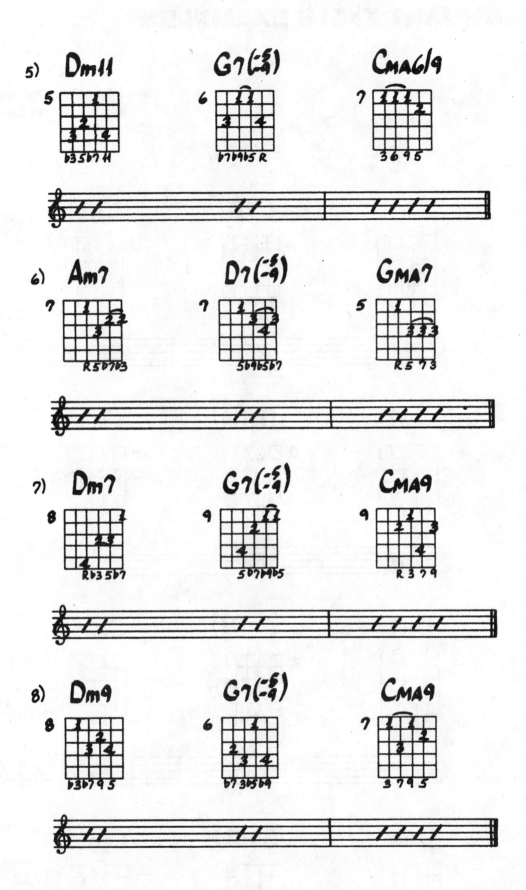

● DOMINANT 7♭5+9

● Keyboard Analysis:

CHORD FORMS

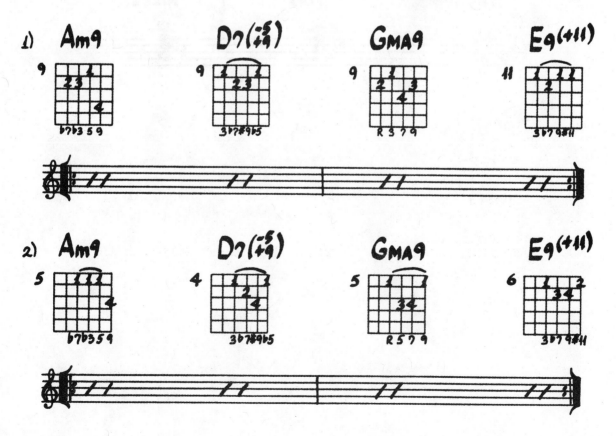

DOMINANT 7♭5+9 EXAMPLES

●● Have a friend play the root note in the bass in order to hear the complete chord.

● DOMINANT 7+5♭9

● **Keyboard Analysis:**

CHORD FORMS

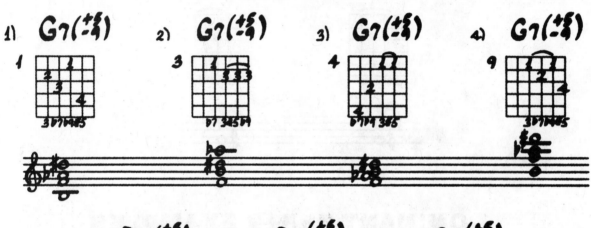

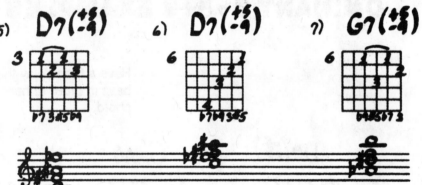

●

•DOMINANT 7+5♭9 EXAMPLES

• • Have a friend play the root note in the bass in order to hear the complete chord.

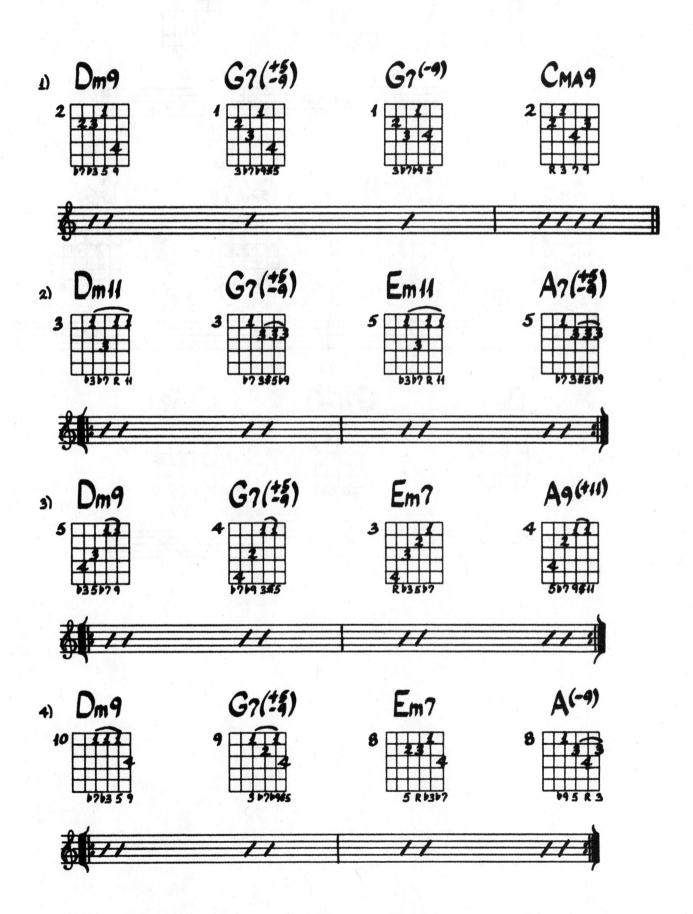

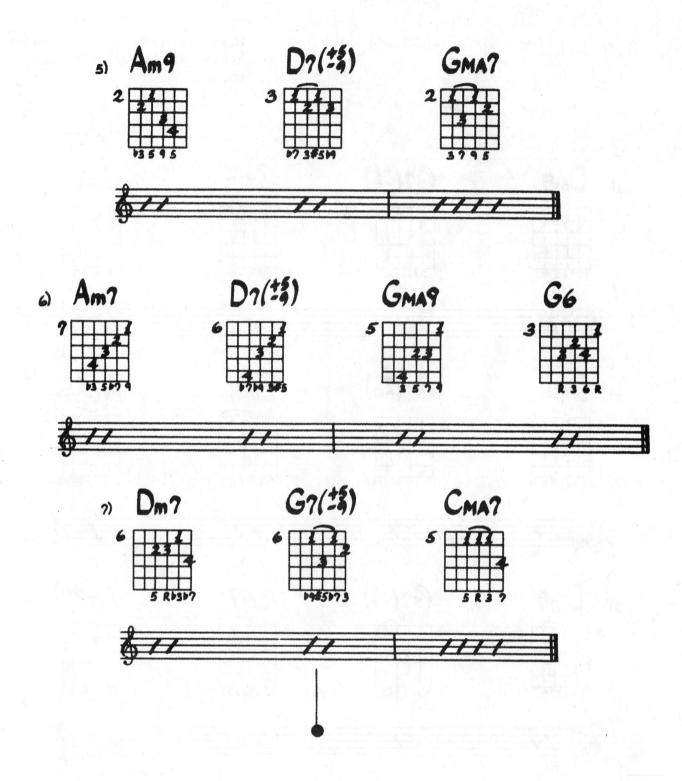

● DOMINANT 7+5+9

● **Keyboard Analysis:**

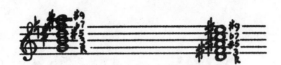

CHORD FORMS

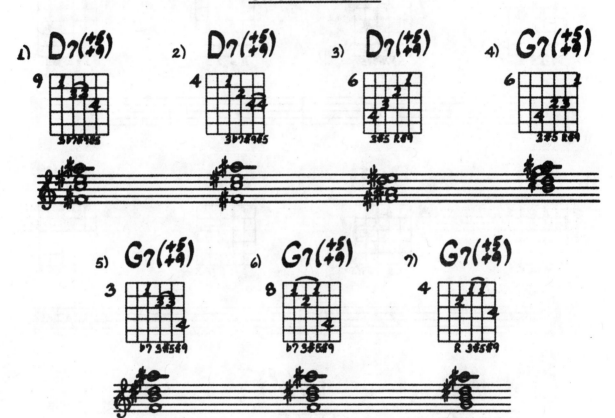

● DOMINANT 7+5+9 EXAMPLES

● ● Have a friend play the root note in the bass in order to hear the complete chord.

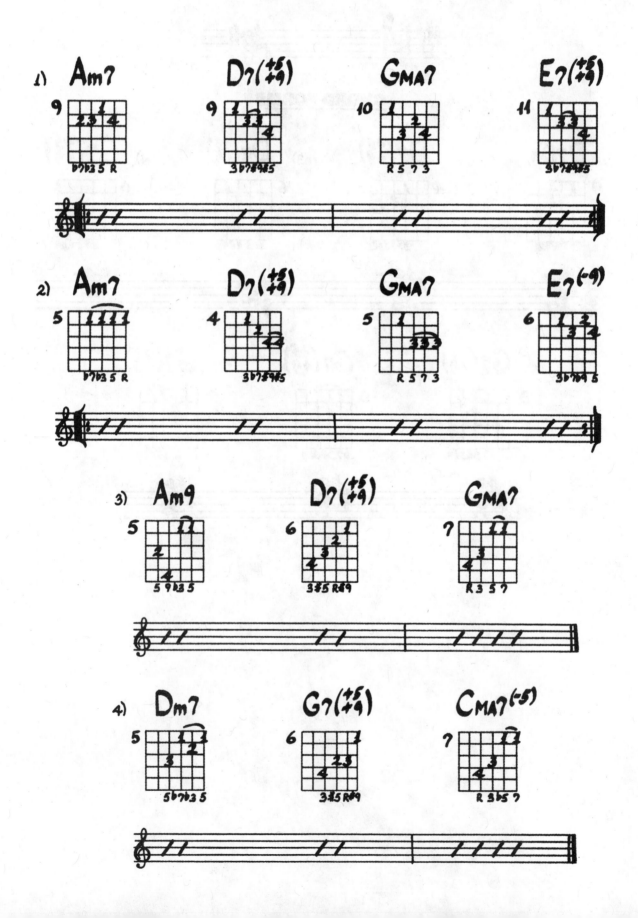

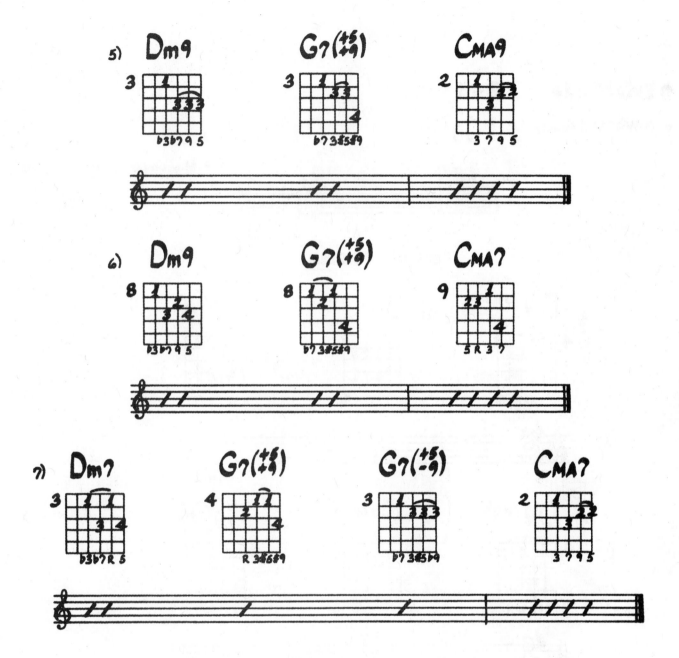

● DOMINANT 9+11(♭5)

● **Keyboard Analysis:** $G9^{(+11)}$ $D9^{(+11)}$

● ● May be considered Dom9♭5

CHORD FORMS

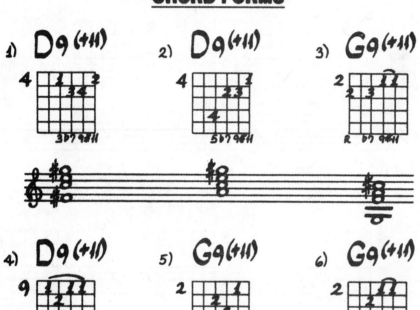

1) $D9^{(+11)}$

2) $D9^{(+11)}$

3) $G9^{(+11)}$

4) $D9^{(+11)}$

5) $G9^{(+11)}$

6) $G9^{(+11)}$

● DOMINANT 9+11(♭5)EXAMPLES

●● Have a friend play the root note in the bass in order to hear the complete chord.

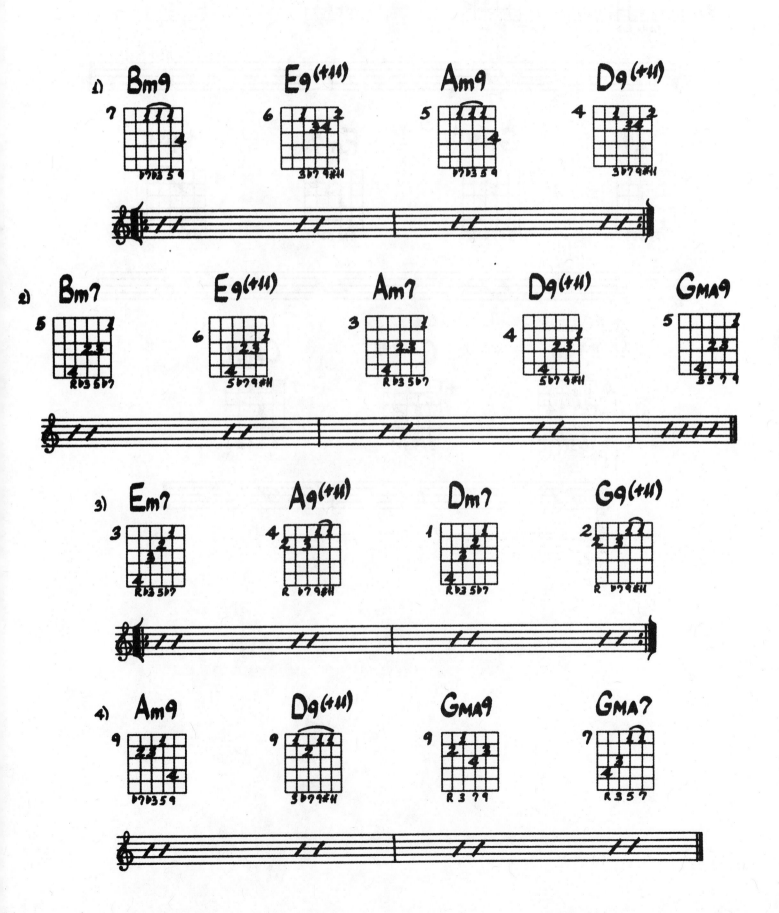

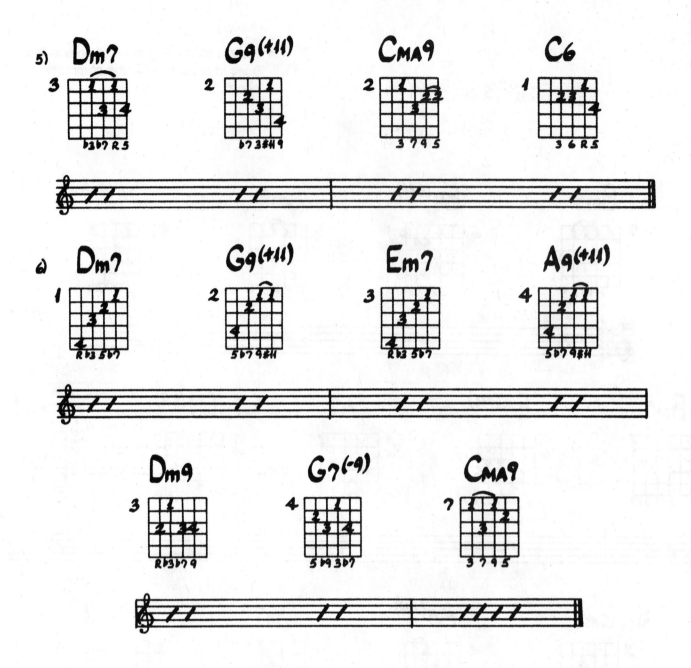

● DOMINANT 9+5

● Keyboard Analysis: G9(+5)   D9(+5)

CHORD FORMS

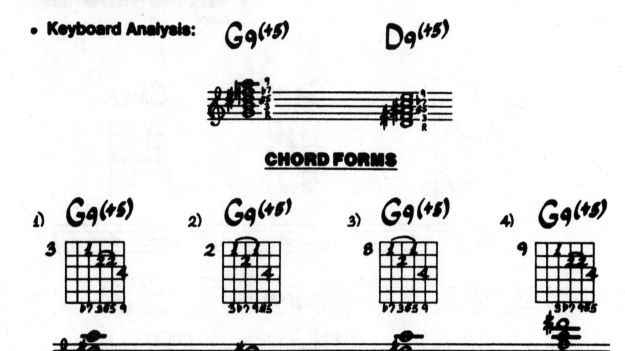

1) G9(+5)   2) G9(+5)   3) G9(+5)   4) G9(+5)

170

● DOMINANT 9+5 EXAMPLES

● ● Have a friend play the root note in the bass in order to hear the complete chord.

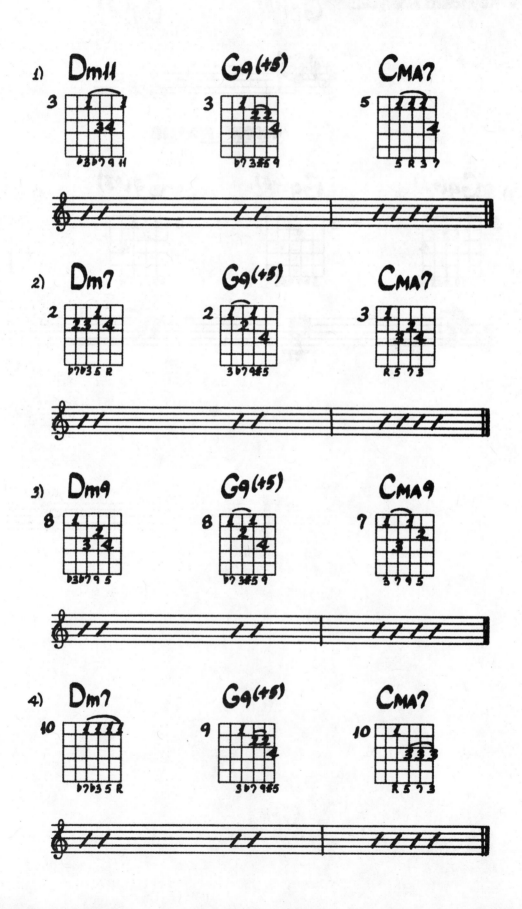

● DOMINANT 11♭9

● Keyboard Analysis:

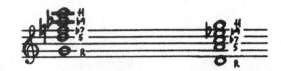

CHORD FORMS

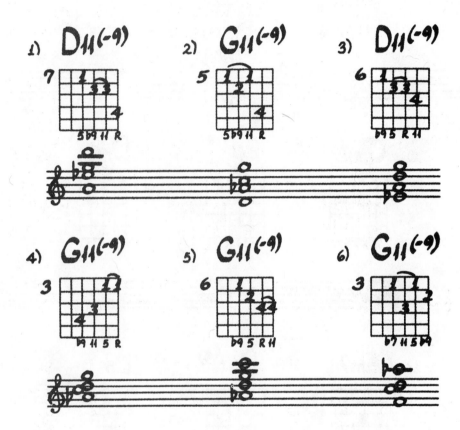

● DOMINANT 11♭9 EXAMPLES

● ● Have a friend play the root note in the bass in order to hear the complete chord.

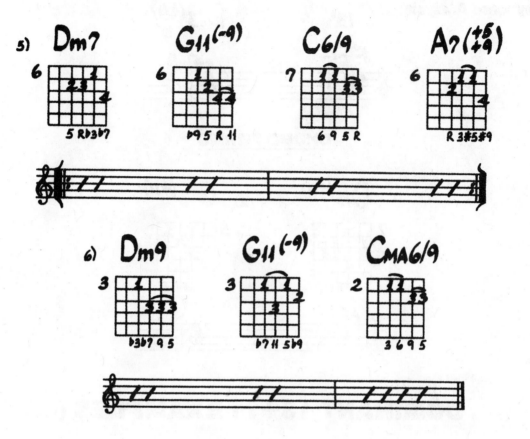

● DOMINANT 13+11 (♭5)

- Keyboard Analysis:

CHORD FORMS

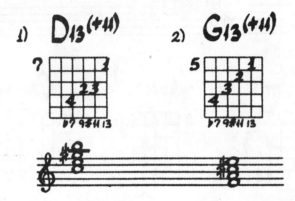

DOMINANT 13+11 EXAMPLES (♭5)

● ● Have a friend play the root note in the bass in order to hear the complete chord.

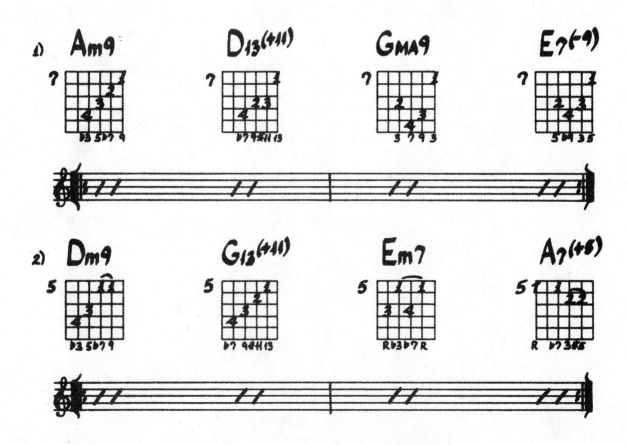

●DOMINANT 13♭9

● **Keyboard Analysis:**

CHORD FORMS

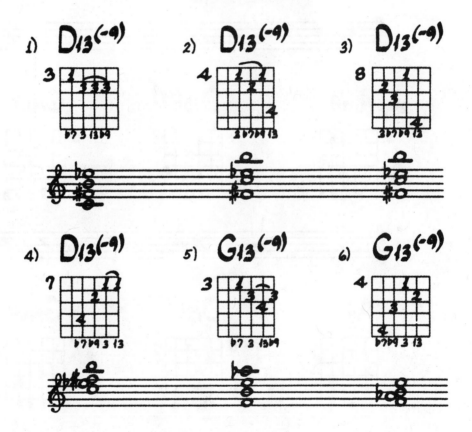

176

● DOMINANT 13♭9 EXAMPLES

● ● Have a friend play the root note in the bass in order to hear the complete chord.

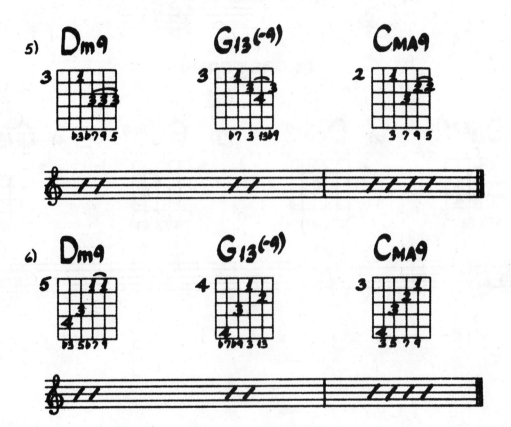

● DOMINANT 13+9

● Keyboard Analysis:

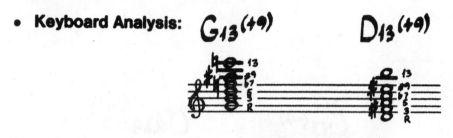

CHORD FORMS

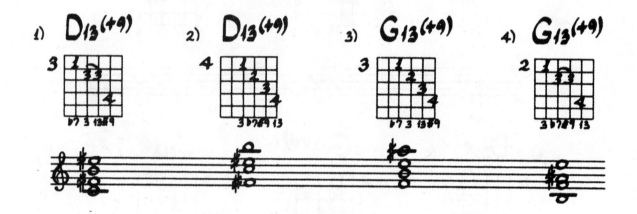

● DOMINANT 13+9 EXAMPLES

● ● Have a friend play the root note in the bass in order to hear the complete chord.

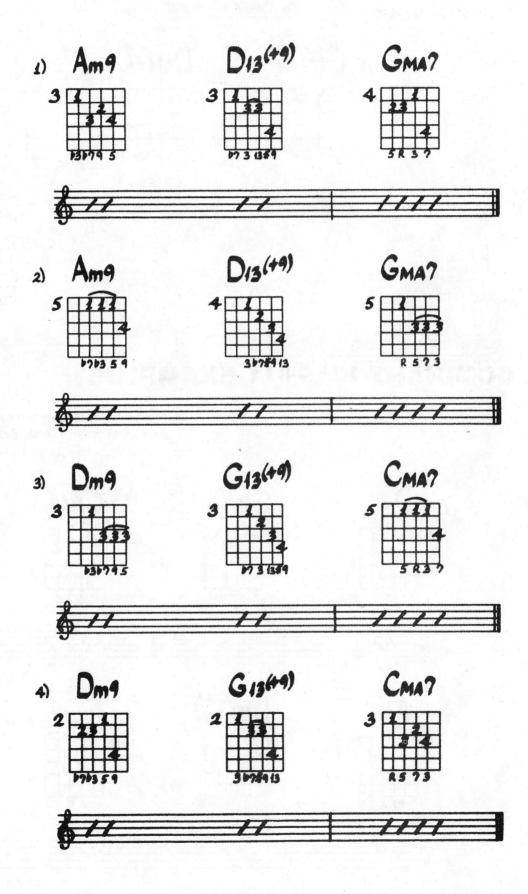

● DOMINANT 13♭9+11

● **Keyboard Analysis:**

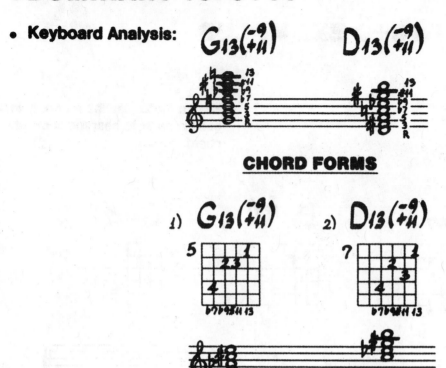

CHORD FORMS

● DOMINANT 13♭9+11 EXAMPLES

● ● Have a friend play the root note in the bass in order to hear the complete chord.

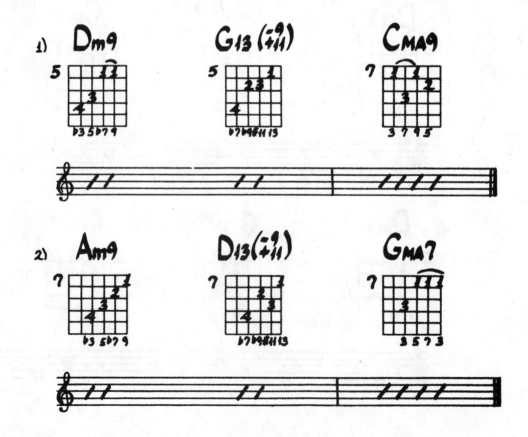

● DOMINANT 13+5+9

● Keyboard Analysis:

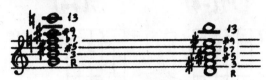

$G_{13}\left(\begin{smallmatrix}+5\\+9\end{smallmatrix}\right)$ $D_{13}\left(\begin{smallmatrix}+5\\+9\end{smallmatrix}\right)$

CHORD FORMS

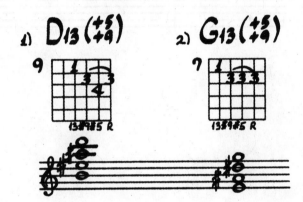

1) $D_{13}\left(\begin{smallmatrix}+5\\+9\end{smallmatrix}\right)$ 2) $G_{13}\left(\begin{smallmatrix}+5\\+9\end{smallmatrix}\right)$

● DOMINANT 13+5+9 EXAMPLES

●● Have a friend play the root note in the bass in order to hear the complete chord.

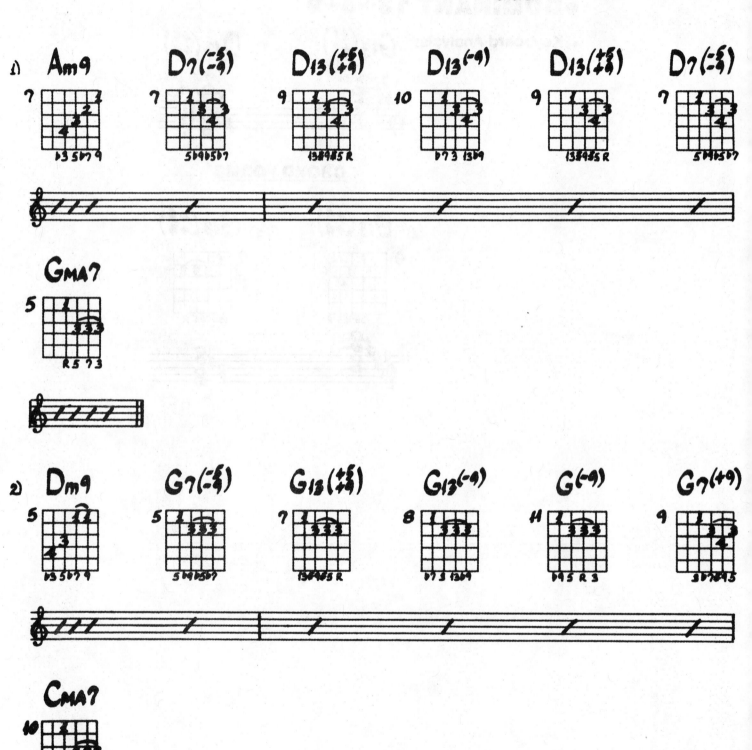

●DIMINISHED

● **Keyboard Analysis:**

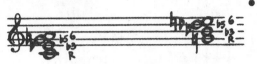

●● Any note in these diminished chords can be considered the root. Diminished forms can also be used as a Dom7 ♭9 chord, i.e. E♭dim = D7♭9 = F7♭9 = A♭7♭9 = B7♭9

CHORD FORMS

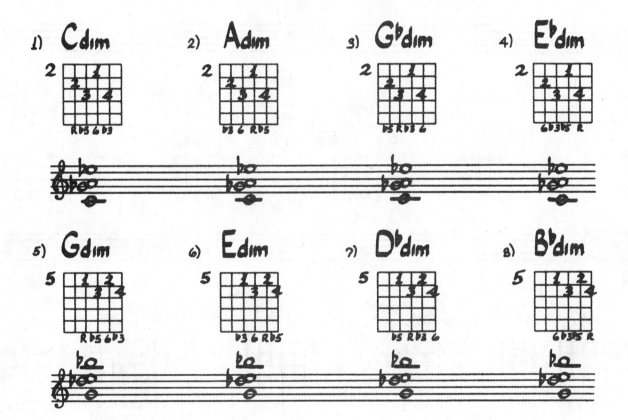

●

184

●DIMINISHED EXAMPLES

● ● Have a friend play the root note in the bass in order to hear the complete chord.

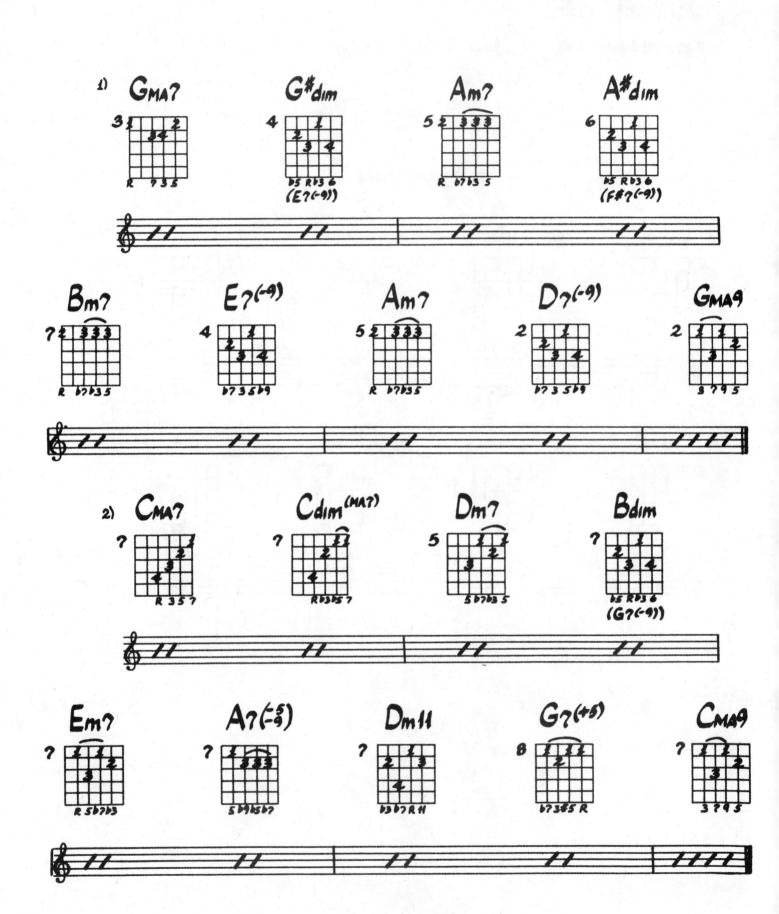

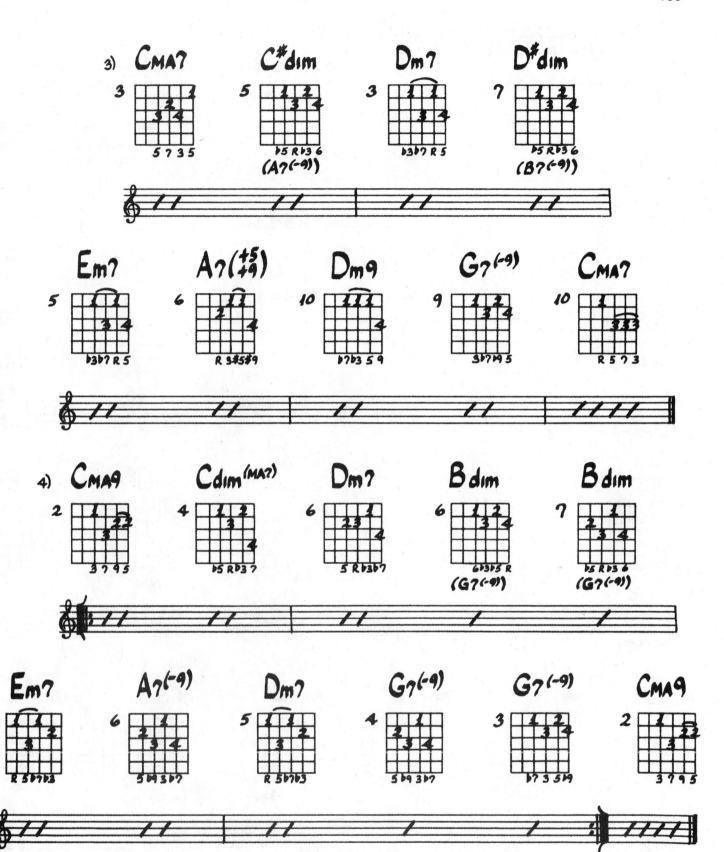

● AUGMENTED

● Keyboard Analysis:

●● See Chromatic Passing Minor-Descending and Basic Major for examples.

CHORD FORMS

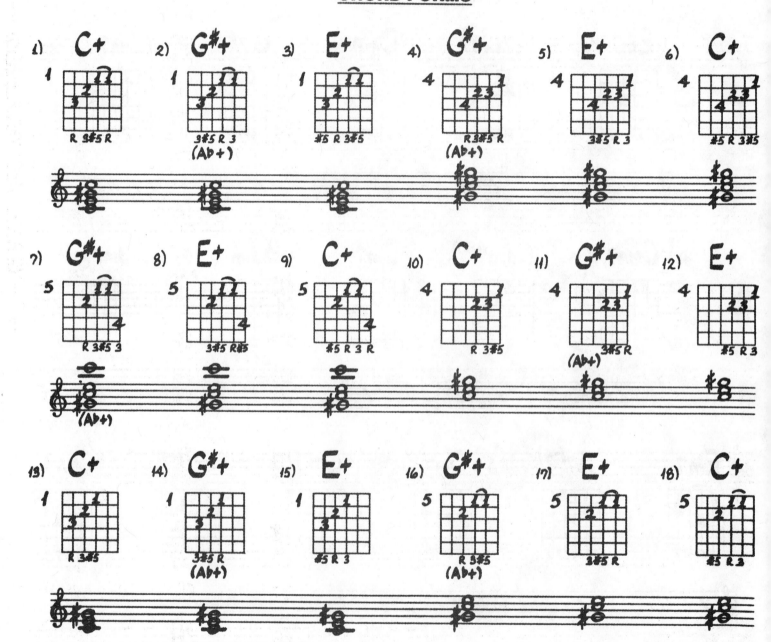

● HARMONIZED SCALES